CONTENTS

PART THREE

CRITICAL APPROACHES Themes

YORK NOTES

SONGS OF INNOCENCE AND OF EXPERIENCE

WILLIAM BLAKE

NOTES BY DAVID PUNTER

Longman

 York Press

The illustrations of 'The Chimney Sweeper' and 'The Tyger' (pages 64 and 70) are taken from Copy R (c. 1802-08) plates 11 and 43, and of 'London' (page 76) from Copy AA (c. 1815-26) plate 46, of William Blake's 'Songs of Innocence and of Experience' and are published courtesy of the Fitzwilliam Museum, University of Cambridge and the Bridgeman Art Library London. All are etchings using ink and watercolour.

The right of David Punter to be identified as Author of this Work
has been asserted by him in accordance with the
Copyright, Designs and Patents Act 1988

YORK PRESS
322 Old Brompton Road, London SW5 9JH

PEARSON EDUCATION LIMITED
Edinburgh Gate, Harlow,
Essex CM20 2JE, United Kingdom
Associated companies, branches and representatives throughout the world

First published 1998
This new and fully revised edition first published 2003
Second impression 2004

10 9 8 7 6 5 4 3 2

ISBN 0-582-78433-6

Designed by Michelle Cannatella
Typeset by Pantek Arts Ltd, Maidstone, Kent
Produced by Pearson Education Asia Limited, Hong Kong

PART ONE

INTRODUCTION

HOW TO STUDY A POEM

Studying on your own requires self-discipline and a carefully thought-out work plan in order to be effective.

CONTEXT

The word 'poetry' comes from the Greek word *poesis*, meaning 'making' or 'creating'. People have been writing poetry for thousands of years – the earliest we have dates back to c. 3000BC.

- Poetry is the most challenging kind of literary writing. In your first reading you may well not understand what the poem is about. Don't jump too swiftly to any conclusions about the poem's meaning.

- Read the poem many times, and including out loud. After the second or third reading, write down any features you find interesting or unusual.

- What is the poem's tone of voice? What is the poem's mood?

- Does the poem have an argument? Is it descriptive?

- Is the poet writing in his or her own voice? Might he or she be using a **persona** or mask?

- Is there anything special about the kind of language the poet has chosen? Which words stand out? Why?

- What elements are repeated? Consider **alliteration, assonance,** rhyme, rhythm, **metaphor** and ideas.

- What might the poem's images suggest or **symbolise**?

- What might be significant about the way the poem is arranged in lines? Is there a regular pattern of lines? Does the grammar coincide with the ending of the lines or does it 'run over'? What is the effect of this?

- Do not consider the poem in isolation. Can you compare and contrast the poem with any other work by the same poet or with any other poem that deals with the same theme?

- What do you think the poem is about?

- Every argument you make about the poem must be backed up with details and quotations that explore its language and organisation.

- Always express your ideas in your own words.

These York Notes offer an introduction to the poetry of *Songs of Innocence and of Experience* and cannot substitute for close reading of the text and the study of secondary sources.

READING *SONGS OF INNOCENCE AND OF EXPERIENCE*

William Blake's *Songs of Innocence and of Experience* (1789 and 1794) occupy a unique position in English literature. Some of them – 'The Tyger', for example – are among the best-known poems in the language; they have been much anthologised, and have been among the favourite poems of many generations. Blake himself was not well known in his lifetime, and his reputation has been through some odd twists and turns, as you will read later in these Notes; but the *Songs* were recognised from the outset as an extraordinary collection, and the contemporary reader will find much in them to delight, as well as much to think about.

One remarkable feature of them is that they stand, in several senses, athwart the mainstream traditions of English literature. Blake is now frequently classed with the **Romantic** writers – particularly Wordsworth and Coleridge, who were roughly his contemporaries – but the *Songs* show little of the high-flown **rhetoric** of the major Romantics. On the contrary, they are often remarkably simple, at least on first reading. They also owe very little to the eighteenth-century **Neoclassical** poetry which preceded them; indeed, Blake's views on his immediate predecessors were often harsh. The major influences on them appear not to have come from the 'official' poetic tradition at all, but rather from more 'popular' sources, particularly from hymns – Blake was in a sense a religious poet, although of a most peculiar kind – and even from children's nursery rhymes.

The *Songs of Innocence* were published first, in 1789, and later as a joint collection with the *Songs of Experience*, which were never published separately. But when we say 'published', we come upon another extraordinary fact about Blake's writing, which is that it was never 'published' during his lifetime in the modern sense of publication; instead, the poems were published by himself, and according to a method which was unique in the history of English writing. For another important fact about the *Songs* is that, in the form in which you will usually find them anthologised or reprinted, they are incomplete, because the actual version of the poems as originally published by Blake was in the form of a book in which each poem occupied a page, or part of a page, which was also 'illuminated'. But these 'illuminations', or illustrations, were

CHECK THE BOOK

Peter Ackroyd's biography, *Blake*, is excellent (see **Further reading**).

much more than that; Blake did not, as it were, dream up an illustration to go with each poem; rather, the poem and the visual material were constructed as a single entity, so that the very meaning of each poem is expanded by, and is sometimes dependent upon, the artwork which originally accompanied it.

CHECK THE NET

Versions of almost all Blake's illuminated books can be found at **http://www.blake.archive.org.**

Each copy Blake made, he made by hand. He was by profession an engraver. What this means is that he lived – and lived often very poorly – by being offered work by other artists, and engraving copies of it for sale. Similarly with his own work, he would make a master copy and then run off copies and colour them by hand to sell or give to his friends; which in turn means that no two copies are exactly the same, although the words remained identical.

Within the *Songs*, some are obviously paired: for example, we find poems called 'The Chimney Sweeper' and 'Holy Thursday' in both the *Songs of Innocence* and the *Songs of Experience*, and it is therefore probable that Blake meant these pairs of poems to be read together, and to act as commentaries on each other. Other pairings have been assumed by critics – for example, 'The Lamb' and 'The Tyger' have often been viewed together, although we have no real evidence from Blake himself that this was meant to be so. To understand these pairings, and to understand the *Songs* as a whole, therefore, we need to have some grasp of what Blake meant by 'Innocence' and what he meant by 'Experience', and this is a question which has occupied critics for many years, and is still very much open to discussion. Here are some questions you might like to think about, and to which I shall return in the pages which follow.

CHECK THE BOOK

Very helpful on these issues is Heather Glen's *Vision and Disenchantment* (see **Further reading**).

What did Blake mean by 'Innocence', and how is it different from ignorance? To whom are the *Songs of Innocence* addressed – are they meant to be read *by* children, or perhaps *as if* we were children? If the state of innocence in some sense corresponds to childhood, do the *Songs of Experience* therefore represent an adult perspective? If they do, then are we to see this adult perspective as a corrective to the childhood view, or as a falling from grace? Is there implicit in the poems a 'third view', as Blake sometimes seems to have said, which is *beyond* both innocence and experience? And where, behind all this, is the *narrator* of the poems, and how can we describe that narrator?

PART TWO

THE POEMS

NOTE ON THE TEXT

Songs of Innocence was Blake's first book. We do not know how many copies of it were made, for he continued to produce copies of his various works throughout his lifetime, depending on demand, but twenty-one copies of the original issue are known to exist now, differing slightly in the artwork, but identical in the wording of the poems. There is more than one way of ordering the poems, and we know that in some copies of the joint work, *Songs of Innocence and of Experience*, poems were transferred between the two groupings, which again raises questions about Blake's view of innocence and experience.

The Songs of Innocence and of Experience: Shewing the Two Contrary States of the Human Soul were first issued together in 1794, but the arrangement of the poems in the *Songs of Experience* series continued to vary until 1815. Twenty-four copies of the original work are known to exist, and although the text of *Songs of Experience* remains the same from copy to copy, the arrangement of the poems differs, and the colouring of the illustrations, or 'illuminations' as Blake called them, becomes increasingly elaborate as the years passed. The arrangement you will find used in this commentary is the one used in William Blake's *Songs of Innocence and of Experience* edited by Geoffrey Keynes, Oxford Paperbacks, 1970, which will provide you with Blake's original illustrated poems. It is always worth asking yourself the question, however: is this really a 'song of experience', or do innocence and experience enter into such a complex dialogue with each other that the distinction becomes hard to make?

QUESTION
In Blake's *Songs*, what are some of the relations between the states of innocence and experience?

SYNOPSIS

There are forty-six poems in all. All of them are short, some very short indeed. All are written in an apparently simple style, and the most usual verse form is the rhymed **quatrain** (stanza of four lines). Blake is unique among major poets in English before the twentieth century in not using the most conventional line, the **pentameter** (five-foot line) which was common to writers from Shakespeare and Milton through to Pope and beyond; the lines he uses in the *Songs* are shorter, typically the **tetrameter** (four-foot line), as he found it in the popular forms of his day (hymns and nursery rhymes, as I said above, but also the **ballad**, which had a very significant influence on Blake).

The poems are meant to convey two different views of human life, the view of innocence and the view of experience. In the state of innocence, we look at things freshly; we look at natural objects and wonder at them, finding in them a child's simple apprehension of beauty. In the state of experience, this vision is darkened by adult fears and anxieties; we begin to ask questions about whether what we see is actually the case, about how there can be evil in God's creation, about the causes of human suffering. In the state of experience, we might say that we begin to feel the effects of **alienation**; this may mean that we see the world more deeply, but it also means that we see and feel it more painfully. Is this perspective a 'truer' one than that of innocence, or merely a further stage through which we have to pass in order to achieve an even higher truth?

SONGS OF INNOCENCE

INTRODUCTION

- The poet sees a vision of a child on a cloud.
- The child instructs him first to play a tune, then sing, then write his poems down.

COMMENTARY

This poem 'introduces' the *Songs of Innocence*, and at the same time it also introduces us to a certain kind of 'innocent' writing, **symbolised** in conventional eighteenth-century **pastoral** terms by the shepherd's pipe.

Blake is very much present as the narrator (the 'I', which occurs in each stanza, including three times in the final one) of this poem; in it, he is asked by a child to 'pipe' songs 'with merry chear' (lines 5-6). It is important to note that the poem itself, with its jaunty rhythms and simple rhymes, is an example of such a 'song' (line 5); even here, amid the apparent simplicity of structure and narrative stance, there is something reflexive about Blake's work, something that always calls attention to itself as an act of writing or inscription.

At the same time, the poem looks forward to the 'Lamb' (line 5) as both a symbol of innocent happiness and also, through its associations with Jesus, as a religious image, thus pointing us towards the complicated arguments about religion which Blake will mount throughout both sets of *Songs*. What is perhaps most interesting here is the duality of reaction in the second stanza. When the 'song about a lamb' is first piped, we are told of the piper's 'merry chear'; but when he pipes again, we are told that the child 'wept... to hear' (line 12), and the reader might reasonably ask what this weeping is about. Although we are told in the third stanza that the child is then weeping 'with joy' (line 12), this might not entirely erase a different impression in the second one, where the weeping might have something also to do with the fragility of the lamb, with a sense that the world of innocence might not be all there is to apprehend and that we need to be prepared for the very different understandings of the world which we encounter in later poems.

And even here, in this apparently most innocent of songs, there is a word which might seem to jar. What does Blake mean by 'stain'd' in line 18? Does he simply mean to refer to the mutual operation of ink (or paint) and water, and thus to the 'water-colour' of his illuminations, or does he suggest here the inevitability that even the act of writing about innocence will taint the subject matter?

 CHECK THE BOOK

For a wide selection of views on Blake, see *The Cambridge Companion to William Blake*, edited by Maurice (see **Further reading**) Eaves, 2003.

THE SHEPHERD

- The shepherd roams freely.
- He is in touch with natural, instinctive love, and has an idyllic life.

COMMENTARY

Like 'The Lamb', this poem plays on conventional biblical imagery of the 'good shepherd', while at the same time adopting the equally conventional poetic identification of the shepherd with the poet.

The shepherd here is an emblem of, among other things, perfect natural freedom; he can, according to this poem and the others in the tradition from which it arises, roam where he pleases, and he is free from the trammels of organised city life. At the same time he is also, like God, an ultimate father figure; we notice that it is the lamb and the ewe who need his protection, and it is on their behalf that he needs to remain 'watchful'. Thus the poem places alongside an image of pure freedom the necessity of remaining ever alert lest this paradisal state of affairs should come under sudden attack.

CHECK THE BOOK

On Blake and the political, see E.P. Thompson, *Witness against the Beast: William Blake and the Moral Law*, 1993.

Perhaps this is, of all the poems in *Songs of Innocence*, one in which Blake is most obviously speaking to children; but not in order to remind them, in didactic fashion, of their 'duty', rather to say how much in need of protection they (and, by extension, all of us) are. What, though, is the precise structure of the last two lines? What might happen if their shepherd were not 'nigh' (line 8)? Is the peace which they experience a temporary thing, destined to be shattered by the coming of a different world, the world of experience, into which we all must at some stage enter?

We might also in this poem want to think about the word 'strays', which concludes the second line. Although this might indeed serve to connote the pleasure of freedom, it might also conjure up the possibility of being lost and thus failing to offer protection - or indeed to be protected. In such other poems of the *Songs of Innocence* as 'A Dream', 'The Little Boy Lost', 'The Little Boy Found', 'The Little Girl Lost' and 'The Little Girl Found', Blake presents us with a powerful array of images of loss and straying; indeed, some critics have seen these poems as particularly oddly placed in the realm of innocence since the dangers they touch upon seem very much to interlock with the world of experience.

- This poem depicts a conventional village scene in which a whole day's cycle is portrayed.
- Within it youth and age all have their parts to play alongside the birds and the other creatures of spring.

COMMENTARY

The old shepherd still has a place in family and society, Blake is saying, even though in the city he might be displaced or pensioned off. Similarly, the artificiality within which city children might be brought up is implicitly contrasted with the 'natural' cycle of the countryside whereby children rest when they are tired and 'sport' naturally ends with the closing of the day.

Blake, as a virtually lifelong Londoner, may well never have witnessed such a scene but it serves him as a contrast to the physically and emotionally polluted environment of the city. The first person plural, particularly in the form of 'our' (line 9) appears frequently in this poem. Who, precisely, is this 'our'? Or is it primarily meant to signify a common sense of ownership, of belonging? The last part of the second stanza consists of a reminiscence by the 'old folk' in connection with the play of the youngsters. Are we meant to see in this a natural development from youth to old age, or should we also see it as a kind of nostalgia? In other words, in what sense does Blake mean us to take this scene of happy harmony as 'real', or is he saying that we need to create, or recreate, such an image, even if it really no longer exists, for our own happiness? There are, perhaps, two slightly disturbing signs that the world of the village green is under threat. The first would arise from a different reading of the last two lines, whereby the idea of sports being 'no more seen' and the green itself 'darkening' might not signify only the natural ending of the day, but also a possible ending of a certain tradition, the coming in of night to

> **CONTEXT**
>
> This notion of the threat to rural life is persistent: compare, for example, Philip Larkin's poem, 'Going, Going'.

GLOSSARY

11 **Old John** a conventional pastoral figure in eighteenth-century poetry

menace our safety and, more importantly, that of our children. The second might occur to us as we contemplate the title of the poem: why is it an 'Ecchoing' green? Is it because it reverberates with laughter and play, or is it because it continues to resound with the 'echo' of something either already or imminently lost?

THE LAMB

- The narrator asks us to relate the lamb's image as the most innocent of God's creatures to the image of his maker, the 'Lamb of God'.

COMMENTARY

Although Blake here invites us to dwell upon the image of the lamb, it would appear that this is not the final purpose of the poem, which is rather to invite the audience to 'use' this image as a means of asking questions about the whole of creation. The insistent question is, 'who made thee' (line 1), and while this might well seem a question most appropriately asked of young children, we should be in no doubt that Blake intends it also as a question he means to address to all the people of his times, and especially as a reminder to those sunk in the travails of war or industrial labour that there remains a more innocent world which we can still see if we allow ourselves to, as he puts it elsewhere, 'cleanse' our 'doors of perception'.

The most puzzling line is line 17: 'I a child & thou a lamb '(line 17). Clearly there are words missing here, words that would be necessary in a 'prose paraphrase': does Blake mean to say that I 'became' a child, and thou 'became' a lamb? Or is he saying more starkly that he, Blake or the narrator, *is* a child, at least for the sake of these poems; and what would this mean for the stance *we* might need to take up when reading at least some of these poems, or, in turn, for the kind of complex interpretations that we might feel obliged to make, interpretations that might be very particular to the 'adult' part of ourselves?

THE LITTLE BLACK BOY

- A little black boy muses on his position in the world.
- He tries to explain both God's purposes and the differences between human beings.

COMMENTARY

This is one of the most clearly political poems Blake ever wrote, and has its roots in the anti-slavery debates of his times. While all the early parts of the poem might seem to suggest that the black boy acts upon his presumed subservience to white ideals, the conclusion magnificently undercuts that, suggesting that the black boy too has his place in the scheme of things, and that the white boy might not be able to bear the presence of God without the protection offered by his black brother.

This is one of the very few *Songs* written in **pentameter**; we might think that this is a measure of the seriousness Blake accorded to the subject, or we might think that it acts as a measure of the **irony** with which he undercuts white pretensions. At all events, it is a deeply poignant poem, showing the lengths to which a black child might have to go to demonstrate that he too is an object of God's love; but the chain of argument Blake uses is unfaltering up to the final stanza.

CHECK THE BOOK

Look up issues to do with slavery in David V. Erdman, *Blake: Prophet against Empire* (see **Further reading**).

What happens then? Should we assume that the acme of the black boy's delight is to be loved by his white sibling? Or rather say that the black boy is providing a kind of education, an education of compassion or pity, evidenced in the way he strokes 'his silver hair' (line 27), as if realising that whiteness (perhaps here meaning unquestioned, angelic 'purity') cannot withstand the scorching force of God's heat? And where should we then decide that the narrator stands? How do *we* feel confronted by this argument in the current climate of race relations?

One of the more remarkable things about the poem is its overall structure. In the first two stanzas, we are being directly addressed by the 'Little Black Boy'; we then have the central three stanzas, in

? QUESTION
How would you defend or oppose the case that the *Songs of Innocence and of Experience* are essentially political?

which he is recalling his mother addressing him, culminating in the final lines of stanza five, where he hear the voice of God (mediated, of course, through the voices of the mother and the boy); and then, in the last two stanzas, we are back with the boy's voice. There are other minor symmetries as well: for example, the double reference to the kiss, which occurs in both halves of the 'frame narrative'. And behind this there runs something which perhaps already we are beginning to see as quite usual in Blake, the use of double-edged **metaphors** – here, for example, the metaphor of the 'shady grove' (line 16), which seems to signify both protection and concealment at the same time. In fact, there is a doubleness of this kind throughout the poem, in the sense that the relation between body and soul is both specific to the little black boy, but at the same time **symbolic** of the general situation of humankind, whose incarnation in the body is a wonder of God while at the same time it keeps us away from the full realisation of God's spiritual power.

THE BLOSSOM

- 'Blossom' witnesses the happiness of a sparrow and sadness of a robin.
- This is somehow joined to Blake's own heart ('Bosom').

COMMENTARY

Blake's sense of the unification of nature is not restricted to the animal kingdom, but also embraces the flowers and all other parts of creation. Here blossom **symbolises** growth and potential, while the two birds symbolise nature.

These two stanzas repeat each other in terms of structure, which makes us all the more able to focus clearly on the difference between the two. In the first, the sparrow is 'Merry'; in the second, the robin may be 'Pretty' (line 7) but is nonetheless 'sobbing sobbing' (line 10). We may take this to mean that nature has room within it for all manner of feelings and emotions, all of which need to be valued as highly as each other, and all of which, more particularly, deserve to find a place 'Near my Bosom', in other words, in the human heart.

Interestingly, where the first stanza uses the imagery of sight - 'Sees you …' (line 4), the second one replaces this by the imagery of hearing. Is this significant? For example, does it suggest to us that, as well as attending to the manifest visual beauty of nature, we also need to listen to its inward voice? If so, then this marks a kind of disjunction in the natural world; what might 'at first glance' appear perfectly happy may also reveal to us, if we attend more closely, that sorrow is natural too, and to understand this will extend the range of our natural sympathies, and thus of our creative imagination.

CHECK THE BOOK
Look at the comments on imagination in Morton D. Paley, *Energy and the Imagination* (See **Further reading**).

THE CHIMNEY SWEEPER

- A child chimney sweep dreams of Paradise.
- Thus he is able to cope dutifully with his work the following day.

COMMENTARY

The social problem which acts as background to this poem, and to its counterpart in *Songs of Experience*, is well put by W.H. Stevenson in his edition of *The Complete Poems* (1989):

> They were often 'apprenticed' (i.e. sold) at the age of about seven; they were brutally and unscrupulously used by their masters, not clothed, fed or washed; while sweeping, they were in constant danger of suffocation or burning, besides the cancer of the scrotum caused by the soot which was literally never washed from their bodies; they were encouraged to steal, and were often turned out in the streets by their masters to 'cry the streets' on the chance of employment, or for mere begging …

This is one of the most disturbing of all the *Songs of Innocence* (for a more detailed discussion of it see **Extended commentaries – Text 1**). The difficulty hinges on the identity of the 'Angel' (line 13); Blake sometimes associated the angelic with goodness, but increasingly as the years went by he connected it with a kind of hypocritical self-righteousness. Which is it here? What do we feel by the end of the poem? Is it right that Tom Dacre should go happily back to work, or has he been deluded by an entirely false

QUESTION
What kind of image of God is Blake criticising in the *Songs*?

sense of 'duty' – misled, that is, by his own 'innocence'? We could see this poem as an exercise in repression, whereby even the most vulnerable and damaged in society can be convinced – wrongly – that they have a part to play despite their exploitation; the question is, does the narrator *know* this, and what is the reader supposed to believe?

THE LITTLE BOY LOST

- A child loses sight of his father in the night mist.
- Following a will-o'-the-wisp, he walks into a fen.

COMMENTARY

This is one of the oddest poems in *Songs of Innocence*; the illustration shows us a boy following a will-o'-the-wisp, with no father present, and therefore we must assume that he is deluded throughout – more thoroughly lost, we might say, than the other lost figures we find in the *Songs*. The innocence of the poem can only reside in the little boy's attitude, certainly not in the world in which he finds himself.

The poem is extremely compressed, pushing into two brief stanzas a story which, we suspect, could easily have been as long as that of the poems we shall come across later about the 'Little Girl'. If we accept the evidence of the illumination, and there is no father there, then we have a poem which entirely reverses the connotations of the lamb and the shepherd; here there is no 'good shepherd', no protector, and yet the little boy does not know this and is rather following a phantom, a ghost which will, we presume, only lead him further out into the 'mire' (line 7).

As with others of the *Songs*, and especially of the shorter ones, our **interpretation** of the poem depends greatly on its ending, in this case, 'And away the vapour flew' (line 8) There are two possible readings of this: one is that the 'vapour' is for some reason dispersed, possibly because of the little boy's tears; the other is that the 'vapour' continues to fly on deceptively before him, leading him into even greater confusion. Which do you think is more likely?

CHECK THE BOOK

There are a great number of different approaches to interpretation to be found in *Essential Articles for the Study of William Blake, 1970–84*, edited by Nelson Hilton, 1986.

THE LITTLE BOY FOUND

- The little boy is rescued by God from the confusions and danger symbolised by the will-o'-the-wisp.
- He is returned safely to his weeping mother.

COMMENTARY

This poem is obviously a continuation of the previous one. The two stanzas are more easily interpreted than those of the previous poem, and they signify a direct opposition between the 'wand'ring light' (line 2) which represents delusion and loss, and the figure of God who represents truth and safety. When God appears 'like his father in white', we may surmise that God is the figure for the good father; whether this means that the child's 'natural' father has failed him – or whether, by extension, we might suggest that all merely natural fathers must do so – is left open for our opinion. It is of interest, though, that the workings of God here are not towards separating the child from natural life, or from his parents; instead, God brings him back to his mother, thus signifying that natural life cannot be evaded or transcended by faith in the divine, even though such faith may help us when we are in extremities of difficulty.

This relates to the fact that when God appears, he is 'like his father in white' (line 4), which suggests to us the importance that Blake attached throughout his life to the thought that the divine, when it appears, does so in the form of other people.

The question of Blake's religious beliefs is complex and difficult; but certainly one of the most important was that God is not some distant, remote figure who lays down the law and delivers judgements and punishments from afar, but is rather in some sense present whenever people interact with each other in loving and caring ways. There is, Blake will often say, a divine seed within us all, and it is up to us to open the inner eye of the imagination in such a way as to perceive that seed and allow it to develop.

'Sorrow' (line 7) and 'pallor' in Blake are important, but in two ways: Blake suggests that we must have sympathy for these

> **CONTEXT**
>
> Also known as 'Friar's lanthorn', the will o' the wisp is a flame-like phosphorescence that flits hither and thither over marshy ground, deluding people who attempt to follow it. It is actually caused by the gases from decaying vegetable matter being spontaneously combusted.

CONTEXT

Other **Romantic** poems, like Coleridge's *The Rime of the Ancient Mariner*, have often been said to move beyond these ethical considerations.

conditions, but he also suggests that they are often produced by delusion about the shape of the world. Should the little boy's mother have felt sorrow; or should she rather have had faith that her son would be rescued by God? Are these moral and theological questions textually central, or does Blake try to open for us a textual field which is in some sense 'beyond' ethical or religious debate?

LAUGHING SONG

- In a woodland idyll, people and wild creatures join together to celebrate the simple pleasures of nature.

COMMENTARY

This is another of Blake's incarnations of an idealised rural life, with 'Mary and Susan and Emily' (line 7) as embodiments of unspoiled girlhood. What is particularly noticeable is how unafraid Blake is of childlike resolutions to his stanzas: 'Ha, Ha, He' (line 8) would hardly have fitted well into the poetry of most of his immediate predecessors or contemporaries.

This poem also evidences the close proximity of the verbal and the visual in Blake; one might take it to be the written record of a visual scene, a merry meal in the country, in perfect weather, where nothing can interfere with the innocent happiness of those partaking. At the same time, one can see it precisely as a 'Laughing Song', as Blake calls it, in the sense that one can imagine it as a song to which people laugh, as they might drink and sing to a drinking song; as an attempt, then, to induce innocent laughter in a world where such laughter is in perpetual danger of becoming for ever absent, or at the very best difficult to achieve.

Rhyme depends, to an extent, on the rhyming words being significant; in other words, poets do not often, as Blake does here in the first stanza, use 'it' as a rhyming word, any more than they would use 'the'. Why does Blake permit himself this usage? Does it work? If it does, why, and what does that tell us about the peculiar tone of the poem? And finally, how might we relate this to the endings of all the three stanzas?

A CRADLE SONG

- The narrator watches his baby sleeping.
- He is reminded of God who became a human child and wept for mankind.

COMMENTARY

This poem may best be characterised as a rhapsody on sleep and innocence. In his encounter with these states, the narrator receives a strong reminder of the divine; which, as I have said above and as we see throughout the *Songs*, can be seen for Blake only in the human form.

Although the subject matter of this poem may seem very simple, the form is in one sense quite complex: although rhythm and rhyme are easy to make out, there is a curiously 'entwined' way in which crucial words – 'Sweet', 'sleep', 'beguiles' – weave their way through the poem. This creates an effect that we might fairly call 'hypnotic'; the connection between hypnotism and somnambulism suggests to us that Blake may be trying to create a poem which in some sense not only describes but also replicates the condition of sleep – and thus of dream. Not, that is, that he is trying to use the poem to 'put us to sleep' but rather that he is suggesting the possibility of a condition of dream as not only the sublime condition of infancy but also as one way in which we can allow our imagination to roam comparatively untrammelled by the exigencies of the outer world, and that this in turn might lead us to an inner sense of the divine, just as the image of the sleeping infant modulates seemingly effortlessly into an image of the baby Jesus. On the other hand, it needs to be said that this is a somewhat passive image of the imagination, a depiction of a realm that Blake was later to name 'Beulah', which is certainly beautiful and restful but which he nonetheless comes to see as inferior to the more active realms of imaginative perception and action.

> **CONTEXT**
>
> Dreams have been of literary interest since the time of the ancient Greeks, but, until Freud, mostly as omens of the future.

The poem shifts gradually from present tense to the past – why is this? Think also about the word 'beguiles' (line 2), which has a range of meanings, not all of them wholesome. Blake clearly suggests that sleep puts a kind of spell upon us, rather as Shakespeare also suggests in, for example, *A Midsummer Night's Dream*; does this poem encourage us to suppose that this state of bliss can continue for ever, or is it intrinsic to the state of innocence that there will be future change, as with sleep we cannot forget the possibility of an inevitable awakening? Why, to put it another way, does 'weeping' gradually encroach on the poem, as it does in others of Blake's poems?

THE DIVINE IMAGE

- Mercy, pity, peace and love are all divine attributes that have a human form.
- We are therefore beholden to respect all forms of human life.

COMMENTARY

The central doctrine of this poem is one to which Blake was to hold throughout his life, namely, that God has a human form; in other words, that there is nothing in divinity or in creation of which we need to be scared, because the whole of God's creation is essentially in human shape, and thus, especially in the state of innocence, we can safely feel that we belong here, and we need to give thanks to God for the safety he has given us.

Mercy, pity, peace and love were cardinal virtues for Blake; we might contrast them, for example, with apparently 'stronger', or at any rate more masculine, virtues such as courage and righteous anger. In this poem, he claims that these are all of human form; but simultaneously he gives us evidence of this by portraying the emotions themselves as **anthropomorphic**. Blake is saying that when we entertain and live by these virtues, then we are doing our best to aspire to divinity; God does not dwell in the deeps of the universe but in the everyday acts of kindness and compassion which link us to each other and to the rest of the sentient universe.

Blake's line about 'heathen, turk or jew' (line 18) is a difficult one for us to read nowadays. Why does Blake use these examples? Is he suggesting a kind of Christian missionary zeal, or is he on the

CHECK THE BOOK

For an expansion of these ideas, see John Holloway's useful study, *Blake: The Lyric Poetry*, 1990.

contrary suggesting that all people, no matter what their beliefs or traditions, have a part to play in the manifestation of divinity in everyday life, whether those parts are seen as equal or not?

HOLY THURSDAY

- A crowd of children flow into St Paul's Cathedral to sing praise.
- The poet pleads for the virtue of pity, lest goodness be lost.

COMMENTARY

'Holy Thursday' was the day on which in Blake's time poor and destitute children in charity schools sang the praises of their benefactors. Here Blake depicts this scene, in the particular setting of St Paul's Cathedral, in a poem of mellifluous rhythm which nonetheless casts up enormous questions about what he meant by innocence.

If we take this poem completely straight, then we see these poverty-stricken children singing their gratitude for the rich benefactors who have rescued them from poverty and starvation. We see also the narrator admiring their abilities, referring to them as 'multitudes of lambs' (line 7) marvelling in the 'raising' of 'their innocent hands' (line 8). We also see, in the remarkable hymn-like quality of the writing, his ability to impersonate the very events he is describing; and thus we may see this poem as a fittingly 'innocent' companion to the furious poem under the same name in *Songs of Experience* which excoriates all charity as the deceptive get-out of a society lacking in any hint of compassion.

But we could read the whole poem **ironically**. What would the evidence be? 'Seated in companies' (line 6) – is this 'free' or 'natural', or does it smack of regimentation? The beadles (traditionally figures of terror) have 'wands as white as snow' (line 3) – is this snow a **symbol** of purity or the chill accompaniment to a regime devoid of pity? The 'angel' of line 12 – is this the good angel we shall come across next in 'Night' or the hypocritical angel of 'The Chimney Sweeper' who persuades Tom, against all the evidence, that all is right with the world?

 CHECK THE NET

See what you can find on the Net about 'charity schools'.

Again we see here the powerful doubleness of Blake's **metaphors**, his insistence – which runs right through his poetry – on performing his own personal revaluations of the moral codes of his society. Even the most apparently innocent of ceremonies or rituals may have another side, and those who may most publicly be seen to be doing good may in fact only be serving their own purposes. Innocence, therefore, is always precarious, always open to exploitation. This does not make it any the less valuable – on the contrary, it underlines the importance of protecting and valuing it whenever it is found – but it does mean that we may need to see beyond innocence and to take into account also the hidden sides of the social order, the purposes which these children are being made unwittingly to serve.

NIGHT

- Night descends and nature sleeps.
- Nature is watched over by protecting angels so that even the lion becomes benign.

QUESTION
How does the imagery of night, sleep and dream figure in the *Songs of Innocence and of Experience*?

COMMENTARY

We might think of this poem as Blake's musing on the biblical phrase, 'And the lion shall lie down with the lamb'; it uses imagery we shall see later in 'The Little Girl Lost' and 'The Little Girl Found', and which we have already seen in 'The Shepherd', to show how in an ideally innocent world (here, perhaps unusually, **symbolised** by 'Night') the lion will take on the protective role previously assigned to the shepherd.

Night here is the realm of the angels; it stands for peace, tranquillity, a transformed world in which all danger will pass away. The angels here are undoubtedly good, which is not always the case in Blake; they are compassionate and protective, and they have the power to turn all of creation in that direction.

The poem uses an unusual verse form: in each stanza the first four lines are alternate **tetrameter** and **trimeter**, while the last four lines are **dimeter;** this perhaps encourages us to read with a mixture of the stately and the joyful, a mixture, for Blake, typical of God's operation in the world.

One of the most interesting moments of the poem occurs in stanza four. Here we find the 'wolves and tygers' howling for prey. The first reaction of the angels is to pity and weep for them. It is not that the desires and needs of the wolves and tigers, unfortunate for sheep as these may be, can be simply ignored or corrected. Rather, each living creature has its own destiny and its own pattern of behaviour, so that, as we see in the second half of the stanza, if the angels' first attempts are unsuccessful then they take up a new role, accepting into heaven each creature as it is slain. These angels are not trying to turn creation away from its own nature; they may try to palliate or alleviate some of nature's more cruel characteristics, but in the end every creature must do what it has to do because it has its own particular individuality.

Sleep, darkness and night are portrayed by many poets and painters as times of danger, as well as times when dreams and nightmares may come. Blake here envisages a totally different scenario for 'Night'; can you describe what this scenario is, and in what ways it follows from the overall vision of innocence Blake is trying to inspire? If we were to envisage the opposite pole of 'day', of what would it consist?

> **CONTEXT**
>
> There is no evidence that Blake ever saw a tiger, though he may have done, since there were menageries in London at the time. There was a particularly famous one in the Strand.

SPRING

- Birdsong, children and a lamb welcome the new year.

COMMENTARY

These three stanzas are very simple, but ideally they should be read in conjunction with Blake's earlier 'To Spring', written while he was very much under the influence of formal eighteenth-century poetry. If we look at the two poems together we see the risks Blake was taking in writing so decisively outside the norms of his times, and in running so close to a poetry *for* children which might have been easily misconstrued as *childish* poetry.

Most of these lines are **dimeters**, a form never used on its own in traditional poetry because it is, obviously, incapable of carrying a great freight of meaning; but here Blake turns it to considerable effect in his conjuring of an innocent, spring-like scene, a million miles away from the 'dewy locks' (line 1) of 'To Spring'. Even the different title is significant; rather than writing an 'Ode to Spring', Blake is here manifesting, as he sees it, the spirit of spring, the simplicity, freshness and newness of the season of birth and childhood.

In the last of the three stanzas, the two protagonists are the (presumably human) narrator and the lamb. Yet it is interesting that it is the narrator who (probably) has the 'white neck' – whiteness being a quality conventionally associated with the lamb's fleece. On closer inspection of the poem, perhaps the distinction between the narrator and the other beings that populate it is not so easy to see – through the device of the **transferred epithet**, we are brought to see that the state of innocence can embrace within it anybody who shares its values.

? QUESTION
Discuss some examples of Blake's uses of the seasons in the *Songs*.

NURSE'S SONG

- The Nurse calls to the children to come home to bed.
- But they, like nature, are still restless on this summer's evening.

COMMENTARY

The first stanza of this poem is evidence of Blake's pleasure in the play of children; thereafter it is a conversation between the children and their nurse, the upshot of which is that the children should be left to the natural cycle of day and night rather than being subjected to the unnatural constraints of duty.

The nurse appears at first to want to tear the children away from their play while they are still enjoying themselves; when the children remonstrate with her, she relents, thus showing all the characteristics of a 'good' nurse in Blake's terms, by recognising their desires and allowing them their freedom at the same time as not imposing any fears on them about their situation. Interestingly, in the second stanza she suggests that 'the sun is gone down' (line 5) - as indeed perhaps it has; but after the children have pleaded with her she accepts that they can continue playing until finally 'the light fades away' (line 13), and at the same time she gives them some responsibility for determining their own lives rather than imposing conventional demands upon them.

The children here can clearly see – perhaps through the eye of the imagination – something the nurse cannot: even though the sun has gone down, they can still see the 'little birds fly' and the sheep on the hills (lines 11 and 12). The strength of the nurse lies in her willingness to realise that their perception may be stronger than her own; it is in this respect, among others, that we need to contrast this 'Nurse's Song' with its bitter opposite number in *Songs of Experience*, where, as we shall see, the nurse is evilly transformed.

INFANT JOY

- The poet addresses a happy newborn child.
- He wishes its joy to continue.

COMMENTARY

This poem states that we are all born in innocence; but it also says that whether we retain that innocence depends on how we are treated, for when the infant says that 'Joy' is its name, the narrator responds in kind by saying 'Sweet joy befall thee' (lines 5 and 6). We could imagine, especially from 'The Chimney Sweeper', a very different response which would blight this little child's hopes of joy in life.

CHECK THE BOOK
Try placing this poem alongside Blake's later poem 'The Mental Traveller'.

This tiny poem seems to speak of an absolute matching between inner and outer life; the infant in need of succour and reassurance receives it directly from the narrator, and we notice here the reciprocity between the child's smiling and the narrator's singing, reminding us once again of how crucial this notion of 'song' is in the poems. Thus we may see the narrator as talking not only about the development of the child but also about the necessary place of song, or poetry, in that development and thus, by extension, in the whole of human life.

It would be perverse to attempt to see a dark side to this poem; but perhaps we might pause to place it alongside 'Infant Sorrow' in *Songs of Experience*, and to reflect on Blake's perception of the enormous differences in the condition of children that he observed, and thus on the complexity of the forces which either allow people to continue to have a sense of childlike innocence throughout their lives or kill that sense off in the very young.

Many critics have commented on the similarities and differences between Blake's views on childhood and those of his approximate contemporary William Wordsworth. More interesting in some ways is to compare Blake with the later novelist Charles Dickens who, in novels like *Oliver Twist* and *David Copperfield*, gives us some of the most powerful images in English literature of the terrors a child can face when treated badly. Blake, obviously, does not give us the same degree of detail as Dickens; but we can still sense in his poems the fearful sense of isolation that a child can experience if his or her needs are not met or understood.

CHECK THE BOOK
On Blake and psychology, see Brenda S. Webster's *Blake's Prophetic Psychology* (see **Further reading**).

A DREAM

- In a dream, an ant loses its way.
- It is rescued by a glow-worm.

COMMENTARY

This poem suggests that it is a 'dream' of the narrator's, and in it he hears about an ant ('Emmet' – line 3) that has lost its way, but is then brought (we suppose) back to safety by the light of the glow-worm.

The characters of this poem, the 'Emmet', the beetle and the glow-worm, are typical of Blake's interest throughout the *Songs of Innocence* in the humblest of all living creatures. It is a condition of innocence in Blake's view that human beings experience their continuity with the whole living universe, and this, as Blake sees it, is also in tune with the Christian teaching on caring for even the least of God's creatures. The poem also speaks of loss, and particularly of the fears of parents – in this case, but also, in other poems, of children – who have been separated from their loved ones and have thus lost their place in the interconnected universe.

Again, this is apparently a very simple poem, and reminds us of the nursery rhyme, 'Ladybird, ladybird, fly away home'. But against this we must place, first, the strong rendition of a condition of fear which is given to us in the second stanza; and secondly, the curious term 'methought' in line 4. Does this imply some doubt about the narrator's position in the poem? In what sense, exactly, is this poem a dream? Or, to put it more broadly, we might ask how we can speak of the status of 'dream' at all in fictional writing since, after all, no piece of writing can offer us 'real things' as they exist in the material, daylight world.

This is a thought which we could pursue through Blake more generally, because he said some very strange things from time to time about his writing, things that played a part in forming the Victorian image of 'mad Blake'. He said, for example, that his writings, and particularly his long 'Prophetic Books', were dictated to him by spirits, so that he was, in effect, merely acting as a kind of secretary to higher powers; he claimed also that many of his ideas came to him in dreams or 'visions'. An interesting comparison is with Samuel Taylor Coleridge, who famously claimed that the poem we now know as 'Kubla Khan' is merely a small fragment of a far longer poem that came to him, whole, in a dream, but most of which he forgot when he was interrupted in the process of writing it down by the notorious 'person from Porlock'.

> **CONTEXT**
>
> In Victorian anthologies, only the *Songs* were usually reproduced.

ON ANOTHERS SORROW

- Can it be possible not to show compassion – in the way God always does – to the meanest of creatures?

COMMENTARY

In many ways, we can see this poem as a summary of much of what Blake has been trying to say throughout the *Songs of Innocence*. It is a poem about the interaction of all life; about how we cannot – or should not – remain immune to the sufferings of others; and about how the figure of God, correctly interpreted, may come to represent precisely that sense of compassion and of respect for all forms of life which should inform all our actions, as it informed our state of being when in the condition of innocence.

The poem is not a narrative; it is a statement of position, a description and advocacy of an ethic, rendered graphic by the passion with which the poet writes. As in some others of the *Songs* (notably 'The Tyger') this passion is conveyed by a series of questions, yet these are not ordinary questions, they are suffused by incredulity; can, Blake asks, anybody conceivably give the *wrong* answer to any of these extraordinarily simple questions? 'Never never', he says, 'can it be' (line 12).

And yet, is that incredulity merely the voice of innocence? For we know, and presumably the poet also knows, that much of the time we – or humanity generally – do not feel instant empathy with those who suffer; perhaps again there is a certain complex **irony** here, whereby we as readers know in one sense that we must agree with Blake while also knowing in another that we frequently act otherwise. Perhaps after all, in this poem as in some others, these kinds of question figure as undecidable; they bring us up against the limits of certainty in language.

QUESTION
Consider the various experiences of 'joy' and 'sorrow' recounted in the *Songs*.

What we might also want to emphasise in this poem is the double emphasis of the actions of God in the final stanza. He 'gives to us his joy', certainly; but he also sits by us and 'moans'. It is not enough, then, for God to be envisaged merely as someone who can magically remove our afflictions; what is more important – and this of course touches very heavily on the idea of Christ as the 'man of sorrows' – is that he can share in and understand these afflictions. Again, we are encouraged to see God not as a remote figure but as somebody capable of sharing our pleasures and pains, and thus of protecting us from loss while at the same time assuaging our loneliness.

SONGS OF EXPERIENCE

INTRODUCTION

- This poem sets the scene for the fallen world that Blake will portray throughout the *Songs of Experience*.

COMMENTARY

It is crucially important to realise from the outset that the 'Holy Word' (line 4) is not really the voice of God; rather, it is the voice of a false creator, who wants man's soul to be satisfied with 'The starry floor / The watry shore' (lines 18 and 19) which are mere distractions from the real life of the imagination.

This 'Bard' (line 1) is obviously very different from the 'Piper' of the *Songs of Innocence*. He does not bring revelation, but preaches a language of 'controll' (line 8), in other words of restriction and constraint. It is essential to Blake's philosophy that each individual contains an inner infinity; to look outward upon the stars is merely to be distracted from the development of this inward human power and to fall prey to the delusions of science. The language of control is thus inseparably linked with the language of 'weeping', 'worn' and 'slumberous' (lines 7, 13 and 15), according to which the soul in a state of experience is really asleep and exhausted, unable to muster the freshness of vision which has characterised the innocent perspective.

Blake's meaning of 'Holy' (line 4) is always worth attention; often it means 'secret' rather than 'sacred', and one of Blake's main critiques of the priesthood is that it tries to hold truth to itself rather than share it democratically with others.

Already, then, we are in a very different world from that of innocence. Principally, this is a question of narrative position, and thus of how we are going to experience these poems as readers. The bard here has heard the Holy Word, but there remains a question about his attitude towards it. Is he here to bear truthful witness to the 'experienced' view of the world, or will he prove to have been

CHECK THE BOOK

A good general commentary on the two sets of Songs can be found in Zachary Leader's *Reading Blake's Songs* (see **Further reading**).

fatally contaminated by it? Can we trust him to expose the evils of experience, or will he turn out to repeat precisely the false arguments that keep the world in subjugation to a false god? Or, indeed, will we find oscillations between these two positions as we read on through the complexities of experience?

EARTH'S ANSWER

- The imprisoned earth appeals for help.
- She wishes that she might be enabled to break free from the restrictive chains of experience and false reason.

COMMENTARY

This poem makes the position much clearer by opposing two languages and thus two perceptions. On the one hand we have the repressive language of 'Stony dread', 'grey despair' and the 'selfish father of men' (lines 4, 5 and 11); on the other we have the by now familiar innocent language of 'delight', 'spring', the 'buds and blossoms' (lines 13 and 17). Blake's argument will be throughout that the imagination is 'chained down' by the force of repressive reason and the moral law, which consists of regulations and prohibitions.

Earth is here 'Prison'd' by the 'Selfish father of men' (lines 6 and 11) a figure in Blake's mythology otherwise known as Urizen; his function is to 'keep people in their proper place', and thus he needs always to restrict the imagination as well as restricting people's political rights. He does this, Blake tells us, because he is 'jealous' (line 12) of human potential and cannot bear the thought that the imagination might be a stronger power than his cherished 'reason'.

Perhaps the most significant feature of the poem's imagery is the opposition between freedom and bondage, or between what is open and what is hidden. For Blake, openness is crucial; when, in the fourth stanza, we read the phrase 'Does spring hide its joy' (line 16),

CONTEXT

The eighteenth century, in Britain and in France, is frequently known as the 'Age of Reason'.

this in turn reacts back on to some of the more complex imagery. As we have already seen, Blake is capable of using the imagery of 'night' in several different ways; here, its close association with the 'hidden' reassures us as readers that we are looking at night's negative qualities, its prevention of open vision and communication, rather than at its restorative powers.

In the last line, Blake refers to 'free Love', and this and other similar references have been the object of much critical debate. Was Blake really an early advocate of free sexuality, or does he mean something much more **metaphorical**? Perhaps there will never be an entirely clear answer to this question, but it is one always worth bearing in mind as your reading of Blake develops.

THE CLOD & THE PEBBLE

- A clod of clay and a pebble discuss the selfless and selfish versions of love.

COMMENTARY

This beautifully structured poem opposes two views of love: the first regards love as a force whereby one gives oneself to and on behalf of the other; the second speaks of a selfish, jealous love which is only really an excuse for the aggrandisement of the self. By putting them in this order, Blake clearly shows which is dominant in the world of experience.

The argument, then, is clear to see; but why does Blake put these words into the mouths of two such unlikely protagonists as a clod of clay and a pebble? Critics have given various different answers, but the most likely is that the clod is above all things soft, it takes the imprint of the 'cattles feet' (line 6), while the pebble is hard, resistant, unchanging, and is thus a fitting emblem for the soul which cannot change or adapt and cannot fully take on the reality of other people, other minds.

QUESTION
What do the *Songs of Innocence and of Experience* have to tell us about the various forms of human love?

The language of 'binding' which we find in the last stanza is very important to Blake as a **metaphor** for the restriction of freedom. Individuals, in the fallen state which represents our usual experience of life, wish to bind others to them and to bind them down, in order to prevent others' freedom; similarly, the 'jealous God' of the fallen world wants to bind people down, and he does so through the force of the material world, which he uses to hide from us the infinite realms of the imagination through which we might otherwise escape from the limitations of the mortal body.

HOLY THURSDAY

- The speaker sees misery and poverty all around him.
- He tries to understand how this can be when nature is bountiful.

CHECK THE BOOK
On Blake's views on British society, see E.P. Thompson, *Witness against the Beast* (in **Further reading**)

COMMENTARY

A counterpart to 'Holy Thursday' in *Songs of Innocence*, this poem provides a bitter view of 'cold charity' and of the society which makes it necessary. Notice how the structure differs from that of its 'innocent' counterpart: the lines are shorter, the poem is full of questions and exclamations, and the rounded rhythms of the earlier poem have disappeared from this barbarous world.

The protagonist of this poem asks questions. In the first stanza he appears amazed that in a 'rich and fruitful land' there can still be chronic destitution; the only explanation he can think of, in the second stanza, is that his initial perception must have been wrong, and that the whole of Britain must indeed be poor, must indeed, as he goes on to suggest in the third stanza, be subjected to 'eternal winter'. The 'trembling' song, of course, is a revision of the song offered in the 'innocent' poem; whereas there, however **ironically**, one was encouraged to see it as a song of gratitude, here it is all too obvious that behind it lies fear and misery.

But what happens in the final stanza? Does the narrator become able to see the situation in its terrible truth, or does he shy away at the last minute, preferring to reside in a fiction, a lie, that what he has been seeing cannot be true? If this is so, what does this tell us about the whole state of experience as a means of repressing unacceptable truths by constructing an ideology which contradicts our own senses?

Part of the difficulty in finding a clear answer to this question hinges on the question of 'where' the action is occurring. 'It is eternal winter there!', Blake says at the end of stanza three; but 'Babe can never hunger there,/Nor poverty the mind appal', he continues in the last stanza. Although it may be impossible to come at a definitive answer, what seems important is that for Blake there may well have been no such thing as a definite, objective location: all depends on perception. Britain may well be both rich and poor – both in the perhaps obvious sense of social and economic injustice and inequity, but also, more subtly, in the sense that all will depend on your perspective. In Blake there is a very complex relation between imagination and the material world. It is not that he naively claimed that anybody could be happy if they tried hard enough, no matter what their material circumstances – that would have been too simple; but he did believe that if the eye of the imagination could be opened the world could be transformed, and that this transformation would be a material, social one as well as a question of perception.

THE LITTLE GIRL LOST

- Seven-year-old Lyca wanders the world, and is lost.
- The wild beasts play around her, then take her to the safety of a cave.

COMMENTARY

This poem is about the relation of the innocence of the little lost girl, Lyca, to the beasts of the forest. Although the lion, leopards and tigers might initially appear frightening, they mean no harm to innocence and indeed can serve to put the girl in touch with an instinctual life which can only be of benefit to her.

> **CONTEXT**
>
> This notion of an 'unconscious life' is one of many ways in which Blake has been held to prefigure some of the findings of Freud.

Lyca's parents may be worried on her behalf, but this is only because they do not understand this essential message.

A long poem by the standards of the *Songs*, 'The Little Girl Lost' is written in **trimeters** which aptly convey the innocence of her vision. All of nature, Blake here suggests, is mutually concerned in care for the innocent and the vulnerable; it therefore follows that although we may have fears and anxieties about the wild (and, by implication, about the 'wild' within ourselves, our unconscious life of desires which perhaps from time to time frighten even us), these fears are simply projections on to an outside world which is, at heart, probably good or, at worst, neutral.

CHECK THE BOOK
On Blake's idea of prophecy, see Morton D. Paley's *Energy and the Imagination* (see **Further reading**).

This is one of the poems which appears in some copies in the *Songs of Innocence* and in others in the *Songs of Experience*, and it is interesting to speculate why. The poem clearly contrasts an 'innocent' perception, that of Lyca, with a more 'experienced' one, that of her parents; what is crucial is that it does not contrast them in direct terms with one being 'right', the other 'wrong', rather the poem asserts an organic connection between the perceiver and the perceived. If one can see the world through innocent eyes, then the world will in some way respond to that perception; this is the transformation, for example, that happens to the lion in stanza ten, when his 'royal' stance of detachment turns into play and gambolling. The lion is, perhaps, simply the sum of the effects visited upon him by the perceiver; or, to put it in more literary terms, he is the sum of the various **symbolic** significances which people have attached to him. There is no 'objective' world of nature: what we see as nature has already been formed by our own preconceptions.

What is the relation between the first two stanzas, in which Blake speaks of himself as he engraves the poem and mentions for the first time the complex issue of the 'prophetic', and the rest of the poem? And at the end of the poem, do we in fact feel wholly reassured that the fate of the little girl is to be awakened to the mysteries of nature, or do we sense a more complex process of sexual awakening?

GLOSSARY
4 **Grave** engrave

THE LITTLE GIRL FOUND

- Lyca's parents search for her.
- They encounter a lion but the 'spirit' leads them to their sleeping daughter, peaceful amid the 'tygers wild'.

COMMENTARY

Lyca's parents are in an 'experienced' world, removed from innocence, and thus cannot initially believe that their missing daughter can be safe while wild beasts prowl around; their journey brings them to the brink of exhaustion, and perhaps this temporary extinguishing of hope is necessary for the lion to trust them by licking their hands, which is a precondition to the appearance of the Christ-like figure of the 'spirit arm'd in gold' (line 36) who shows them that their daughter is no longer 'lost' but has joined a different, perhaps more 'natural' kind of life.

A crucial stanza here is the fourth one. Here Blake says that 'pale through pathless ways/The fancied image strays', but this does not truly represent Lyca who, we know, is safe, protected by her innocence. The 'image' is instead the projection of her parents' fears; this is how they see her in their minds' eye. It is noticeable that this 'image' is 'pale', and this has at least three meanings. The pallor represents what her parents imagine to be her weakness and fear; it also represents the pallor of death, which is obviously their principal anxiety; but it also represents the pallor of an image that is not truly from the imagination, and thus does not possess real vividness. Real imagination would enable the parents to see Lyca as she truly is; this image instead is merely 'fancied' (line 14). The **Romantic** poets, Coleridge particularly, were concerned to differentiate between fancy and imagination: the former was seen as an inferior faculty, more like our modern understanding of the term 'fantasy'. Imagination, on the other hand, rested on real empathy with the other, the quality that John Keats wrote about, for example, as 'negative capability': it was not 'imaginary' in the simple sense, but rather represented the true ability to see the other from within, and thus formed, for Coleridge as well as for Blake, the basis of the finest poetry.

 CHECK THE BOOK
The crucial Coleridge text here is *Biographia Literaria*.

This poem follows from the previous one. Although the message is again apparently heartening, and daughter and parents are reunited, the last stanza nevertheless strikes a discordant note when we read that they dwell 'In a lonely dell' (line 50) They have, perhaps, seen the truth about the interconnections within the world of nature; but their 'experienced' understanding does not permit them to return to their previous life. How might we relate this to Blake's own sense of being isolated because of his 'visions' – which might, after all, represent some kind of truth but which might nonetheless be unrecognisable to his potential audience, thereby condemning him too to life 'In a lonely dell'?

THE CHIMNEY SWEEPER

- The narrator asks the chimney sweep where his parents are.
- He tries to explain why they have abandoned him to misery.

COMMENTARY

Again a counterpart, or 'contrary', to the poem in *Songs of Innocence*, this poem presents us with a child sweep trying to explain to a questioner – and no doubt also to himself – how it can be that he is reduced to such misery and pain. The force of the scene is heightened by being placed in winter, amid 'snow' (line 1), emphasising the cold-heartedness of the everyday world of experience.

This poem savagely exposes the hypocrisy of conventional religion; the father and mother are praying while their child is abandoned to the elements. It is also savage about how we mistake children's emotions: because the young sweep might appear happy, in the sense that he is making the best of his dreadful situation, his self-serving parents choose to believe that they have done him 'no injury' (line 10).

QUESTION
Discuss 'jealousy' as a key idea in the *Songs of Innocence and of Experience*.

But again, the poem raises more questions than it answers. For example: the child seems to believe that his earlier happiness was the direct cause of his abandonment, with the implication that in this 'jealous' world such happiness must always be crushed. But is his version of events the right one, or is he also a victim of the paranoid perceptions of experience? Whatever the answer, the fatal inverted trinity of 'God & his Priest & King' (line 11) will remain, throughout Blake's poetry, the overarching sign for a tyranny which is typical of the world of experience at theological and political levels.

The phrase 'weep, weep' (line 2) conjoins two realms. On the one hand, as a contraction of the word 'sweep', it represents the actual cry of child sweeps going about London to find business; on the other, of course, it refers us to the genuine 'weeping' which is the real inner condition of these exploited children, and which ought, by implication, to be our reaction to hearing of their plight. The cry, then, represents indeed the 'notes of woe'; and the 'clothes of death' (lines 8 and 7), while **symbolically** representing the doom of child sweeps, who tended to die young for reasons that are all too obvious, also represent more simply the black clothing – blackened by soot and poverty – which such children would have worn. Here as elsewhere Blake takes everyday phenomena of his time and links them to his wider picture of the emotional state of the world.

> **CONTEXT**
>
> God and Priest and King were frequently the major rhetorical objects of revolt in Europe during the years of and after the French Revolution.

NURSES SONG

- The nurse hears the voices of the children.
- She is only able to relate to them in terms of fear, anxiety and repression.

COMMENTARY

Whereas the earlier 'Nurse's Song' showed a benevolent nurse, responsive to her children's needs and desires, this much shorter and chokingly bitter poem shows a nurse who finds in her charges merely the expression of a potential freedom that she cannot bear to contemplate, and which she must repress at all costs.

The word 'green' suffers a change in the poem: the 'green' of line 1 is still the play space of the children, but when the nurse's face turns 'green' in line 4 we may read this as either a sickness she feels at the sight of the children, or as the mark of her jealousy of their freedom. She cannot apprehend the joy of the children; she only sees play as a waste of time, and as necessarily useless in the face of a future adult life in which desire will always need to be 'disguised'.

What part in all this do the nurse's own memories play? Clearly the days of her youth do not signify the memory of a happy time which she might also encourage in the children; on the contrary they fill her with loathing, and so we might surmise that the repression to which she subjects the children is something she has herself also experienced. Therefore the process of repression goes on down the generations, in a twisted travesty of the nurturing which the nurse is supposed to provide. Then again, what should a nurse's role be? Where are the parents in this poem? Have they too 'gone up to the church to pray'?

The idea that parents, nurses, or any of those in charge of young children tend to revisit on them the suffering they have themselves undergone – or feel themselves to have undergone – is an essential part of Blake's picture of the world. For a valuable further example, you might want to look at the complicated poem called 'The Mental Traveller', which was never published during Blake's lifetime but was found in a manuscript of his now known as the Pickering manuscript. This is a lengthy **symbolic** account of how suffering is passed down through the generations, and of how parents feel it necessary to keep their children under control by means which they will then go on to use on their own children in a cycle of repression and violence.

THE SICK ROSE

- The speaker wonders at the secret destruction of the rose by the 'invisible worm'.

CHECK THE NET

Look up on the Net for other examples of roses in English poetry.

COMMENTARY

This rose might be seen as the contrary of the 'Blossom' of the *Songs of Innocence*. Far from presenting an image of freshness and beauty, it reminds us of sickness, death and decay. The 'worm' (line 2) - which might also be a serpent - is destroying the rose from within, as jealousy and fear, in the world of experience, perpetually destroy our hopes for a better life.

The worm certainly seems, nonetheless, to represent a kind of love; but this is the 'dark secret love' (line 7) which is intimately linked to jealousy and possessiveness, the kind of love that seeks to appropriate the other and in the end to destroy it. There is a kind of 'coming together' of the rose and the worm here, but it is a matter not of sharing and mutual respect but more a sadomasochistic relationship in which what at first appears loving is revealed as a fight to the death.

It is of course significant that Blake chooses, of all flowers, to use the rose here as his **symbol**. Traditionally the rose has stood within the English literary tradition for love; for purity; for beauty; and also for something peculiarly English, becoming a type of national symbol. Whether Blake had all these meanings in mind is something which we shall never know; but certainly his argument gains force from the proximity of the rose and the worm, the apparently pure flower and that which corrupts and stands for death. That which might appear pure on the surface is in fact inhabited by something quite different; this idea reinforces Blake's general argument that it is necessary to look, not at the outer world's appearances, but at the inner life of things in order to discover the imaginative truth.

Why is the worm 'invisible' (line 2) and why does he fly through a 'howling storm' (line 4)? Perhaps the invisibility is to do with the secrecy of this (sexual) liaison, and the storm signifies a kind of passion; but this passion is in the end destructive and self-destructive, the very opposite of the kind of 'free love' that Blake regards as the greatest of all human gifts. The poem is heavily loaded with sexual imagery, for example the 'bed / Of crimson joy' (lines 5-6); this is true of much of Blake's poetry, although there is always a sharp contrast between the imagery of mutual love and the imagery of violence.

THE FLY

- The narrator brushes away a fly.
- This leads him to meditate on his place in the natural order of things.

CONTEXT

Blake's reputation suffered from an assertion, for which there was never any clear evidence, by his first biographers, that he had once been seen with his wife naked in his garden.

COMMENTARY

This is one of the most puzzling of the *Songs*. The narrator
'thoughtlessly' brushes away a fly, and this makes him muse on
whether he too is merely a 'fly' (line 6) in the wider scheme of
things, just as subject to random accident and to the dictates of
mortality. The pleasures of life, therefore, are only temporary; we
are at the mercy of greater powers.

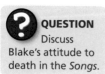

QUESTION
Discuss
Blake's attitude to
death in the *Songs*.

The last two stanzas, however, seem to introduce a new
consideration; for what the narrator appears to be saying is that he
too will be content to be a fly if the alternative is to spend his time
thinking. The poem might therefore be taken to advocate after all a
'thoughtless' way of life, and if this is so we can see why, despite
first appearances, it is placed in the *Songs of Experience*, since this
hedonistic view runs contrary to Blake's frequent advocacy of a
strenuous mental and imaginative engagement with the world.

But we need to consider also the fact that the fourth stanza, which
does not in any case seem to fit well into the poem, is a late
addition. What difference would it make if the stanza were
removed? Would it make the poem clearer, or even more baffling?
More important, would it in fact *change* the meaning of the last
stanza and render it less implicitly critical of the narrator, who
might now be interpreted as practising a courageous stoicism in the
face of the inevitability of death?

In a curious way, it is the very simplicity of the poem that makes
these arguments so hard to be certain about. As in so many of the
other Songs, particularly the *Songs of Experience*, we are required
not merely to interpret a scene or an action, but also to move
beyond or behind this scene or action in order to try to understand
the position of the narrator. The fact is that there may be no clear
answer: the question of how we interpret the poem will itself be a
function of our own situation within the opposites of innocence
and experience. Indeed, we can go one stage further and say that
our reading of poems like this may well be dependent on factors
that change within our own lives, so that we may see such poems
as different upon different readings. This is to say that, as I am sure
is well known, there is no simple or absolute answer to such

questions; but on the other hand, it is important to remember that it is possible to be articulate in our arguments about them, and this imaginative articulacy, this reflection on our own involvements and attitudes and how they colour our vision of the world, seems to have been something that Blake was specifically concerned to produce in his readers.

THE ANGEL

- In a dream, the poet becomes a young girl who, although wooed by an 'Angel', rejects him.
- He finds that when he returns it has grown too late for the prospect of love.

COMMENTARY

This is one of Blake's 'good' angels; the story of the poem is of a 'maiden' line 2) who is loved but is too fearful to respond to the Angel's love, even though he wipes away her tears. She hides her 'hearts delight' (line 8) from him; when he has gone, she wants to experience his love again, but the only way she can do it is through 'arming' herself, and by the time this process is completed everything is too late.

This is one of many of Blake's poems in which he criticises – even **satirises** – the high valuation placed on 'virginity'. The girl believes it is her role in life to keep herself 'pure' and hidden, both literally and **metaphorically**; she can envisage love only as a battlefield on which she must protect what is hers, but her pursuit of this belief leads to disaster.

Again the emphasis here is on the 'hidden', and on the way that what is kept hidden comes in the end to infect the whole organism. This touches also upon the fact that in the *Songs* there are two very different views of 'protection': there is the protection which can be justly offered by God, and sometimes by parents and nurses, and there is the 'over-protectiveness' that prevents one from contact with others. This over-protectiveness is associated with a particular view of the self, as something which is precious and to be kept

> **CONTEXT**
>
> Female virginity was a huge topic in eighteenth-century literature; see, for example, Samuel Richardson's novels, *Pamela* and *Clarissa*.

hidden, secreted away: this process, Blake believed, in the end prevents any real imaginative communication. For such communication to proceed, it is essential that the barriers between self and other be broken down, so that one can see other people, and the world as a whole, in all their glory; otherwise one runs the danger of remaining confined within one's self until, as in this poem, the terrible realisation that old age – and eventually death – have come upon one before one has properly lived.

By virginity, Blake did not only mean physical chastity; he meant also the placing of an over-high valuation on the hidden, protected self, such that any attempt to enter into a relationship gets reconstrued as an invasion, a persecution, a battle. This again is the voice of experience, and the opposite of the innocent perspective, from which one can 'give oneself freely' without fear that such giving will result in the loss or destruction of the self. One of the most difficult lines in the poem is line 4: 'Witless woe, was neer beguil'd!' (line 4). The problem is that the line is compressed: how would you write it in fuller form? Or, if you would find this impossible, why?

THE TYGER

- The poet addresses the 'tyger'.
- He seeks to find out what divine purpose it serves.

COMMENTARY

Perhaps the most famous of all Blake's poems, 'The Tyger' has sometimes been seen as offering a 'contrary' to 'The Lamb'. Centrally, it asks a question about creation: how can we understand a God who is capable of creating the innocence of the lamb and the fury of the tiger?

QUESTION
Take 'The Tyger' as a starting-point for a discussion of what Blake has to say about creativity in the *Songs of Innocence and of Experience*.

But the question is more complex than that, because at the same time Blake is suggesting an equivalence between divine creation and the human creation of the artist/poet who 'frames' the tyger. For Blake, as for Coleridge, there was little difference: the activity of the human creator is a version of divine creativity, and the artist has to be daring, to take risks, in order to produce images of supreme importance to humanity.

My longer comments (see **Extended commentaries – Text 2**) suggest some questions about 'The Tyger'; here, perhaps, the most important thing is to ask, how does the poem fit into the *Songs of Experience*? For by now it should be clear that there are various different ways in which 'experience' informs the poems: in some we are shown the 'world of experience'; in others we are confronted with a narrator who speaks with a 'voice of experience'; in others again we find dialogues in which the principles of experience are more or less subtly undermined by competing voices which remind us of worlds outside experience's domain. Are any of these positions true of 'The Tyger', or must we look for a different solution?

MY PRETTY ROSE TREE

- The narrator is offered a flower.
- He rejects it because he already has a rose tree, but subsequently all his rose tree will give him are her thorns.

COMMENTARY

This poem seems to have a fairly simple **allegorical** meaning. We may assume that the narrator, in a happy relationship with a partner (the 'Pretty Rose-tree') is approached by another woman but rejects her advances; but this produces, not a continuation of their love but rather a situation in which the partner turns away from him 'with jealousy' (line 7).

Why should this happen? First, it happens *in the world of experience*, in other words, in a world where even the threat of jealousy is enough to sour a situation because the fallen mind continues to dwell in its own fears, which eventually totally erode trust between people. Because in the world of experience we all feel guilty, even about our own thoughts, mere abstinence from action will not help – we remain sunk in selfishness, in regrets and terrors about what *might* happen, or have happened.

CONTEXT

Some critics have said that this poem reflects an episode in Blake's relations with his wife.

What is most remarkable about this poem, though, is the apparent contrast between its painful subject matter and the lilting quality of the verse. It is as if Blake were saying to us that, so distorted is the world of experience, even when we come up against its restrictions and perversions we cannot look at them head-on but must instead avoid them. After all, the poem ends up with the word 'delight'; although the obvious meaning of the last line is that there is no delight to be had, might there nonetheless be here a hint of a perverted delight in pain characteristic of experience?

As in 'The Sick Rose', the fact that it is a 'rose tree' that figures here is significant; here the significance resides in the rose tree's conjunction of beauty and pain, the flower and the thorn. This is hardly a new connection, but Blake draws the co-presence of flower and thorn exceptionally tight. Another question one might address to the poem is: what is the role of 'experience' here? It does not seem that we are being talked to by an 'experienced' narrator, but rather, in this case, that we are being shown something about the bitter fruit of experience. But even here there is an ambiguity: are we meant to blame the woman for turning away from the narrator, seeing her as unreasonably jealous and selfish, or are we rather to see her as merely acting in an ideologically programmed way, as the victim of a set of socially imposed beliefs that gives her no choice but to react conventionally?

> **? QUESTION**
> What light does 'My Pretty Rose Tree' throw on Blake's attitudes to the relations between the sexes?

AH! SUN-FLOWER

- The sunflower follows the sun.
- It is seen as an emblem for life's weary traveller who wishes to find heaven.

COMMENTARY

There is a mythological background to this poem, concerning a jealous woman who was turned into a sunflower after her death, but as always Blake converts this material to his own uses. The sunflower is a figure for constant yearning: as it continually turns to face the sun, so it experiences the impossibility of ever moving or changing, so that its earlier jealousy is seen to have made it forever incapable of following its own desires.

The youth and the virgin, as figures in the myth, are similarly incapable of acting out their desires – they are 'bound' in a false 'virginity' – except in 'that sweet golden clime' (line 3) which, despite its attractive description, is the land of death. In that land they may eventually be able to pursue their longings, but only as ghosts, beyond bodily form.

The circularity of form of this poem, beginning and ending with the sunflower, provides evidence of one of the principal attributes of the world of experience, namely that it is a circular world, from which there is no real escape and in which we are condemned, because of the death or absence of the imagination, endlessly to revisit the same situations, the same scenarios of jealousy and torment. Although the poem appears to provide us with a kind of resurrection, for Blake this type of afterlife is no substitute for pursuing one's desires here below: indeed, the very promise of an afterlife is simply an evil god's excuse for his own tyrannical rule.

We might also refer back here to the concept of 'fancy', which I have mentioned before. On that occasion I said that fancy was regarded by the **Romantic** poets as an inferior faculty to the imagination; but in Blake the contrast is even more stark, because fancy, or fantasy, saps one's power to live in the real world. To live in a world of mere fancy is, in one sense, a final example of the many images of being lost that run through the *Songs*: instead of using the imagination to transform natural objects, the operation of fancy abandons the world entirely and leaves one only in the company of ghosts and shades. In this sense while the imagination prefigures life and makes it come into being, fancy prefigures death and makes us lose our bearings and our will to live strenuously and actively.

QUESTION
What ghosts can you identify in the *Songs*?

THE LILLY

- The rose and the sheep exhibit threats.
- They are contrasted with the absolute purity and gentleness of the lily.

COMMENTARY

This highly compressed poem appears to contrast, among other things, the rose and the lily; possibly the 'Pretty Rose-tree' was also in Blake's mind, as a **symbol** of how certain kinds of love can all too readily turn into their opposite, just as the sheep and the 'horned' ram are equally manifestations of the same animal. In contrast to this, the lily, if it represents 'true' (as opposed to false, virginal) purity, has no 'thorn' or 'threat'.

If this is the correct interpretation, then it is at first glance a little difficult to see why the poem has been placed in the *Songs of Experience*, more so when we consider that the connotations placed on whiteness and paleness have not heretofore seemed very positive. Perhaps, however, Blake merely means to call attention to the contrast between the 'thorned' world of experience and the innocent world of purity.

What would happen to the poem, however, if we were to feel suspicious of the image of the lily? This would entail regarding the lily, not as a representative of true purity, but rather as an emblem for the closed self which cannot admit to another side to its nature, and it would take its place among Blake's images for repressive virginity. How convincing do you find such a reading? How might it alter the emphasis we place on the words 'modest' and 'humble' in the first part of the poem?

THE GARDEN OF LOVE

- In what used to be a garden, a chapel has been built.
- What used to be a place of freedom and pleasure has therefore now become a graveyard.

CHECK THE BOOK

Bronowski's *William Blake and the Age of Revolution* (see **Further reading**) provides a broadly Marxist view of Blake.

Here Blake takes up the arguments we have already seen elsewhere in the *Songs of Experience* against 'priesthood'; these priests serve to stifle desire, they act on behalf of Urizen to bring everything under their control, and in the process they convert the innocent 'Garden of Love' into a 'Chapel' (lines 1 and 3) governed by laws and prohibitions which succeed in turning Eden into a graveyard.

Here again we have the image of the 'green' (line 4), the playing space of childhood, subjected to law and order. In one sense Blake is describing the perpetual transition from the freedom of childhood into the restrictive world of the adult, and he is therefore implicitly advocating a world in which that sense of freedom can be allowed to continue into adult life. If this does not happen, then the 'flowers' (line 10) will all wither, or perhaps turn into 'briars' (line 12); the openness of the 'green' (line 4) will be replaced by the 'shut' (line 5) gates of the chapel, a 'holy' place in Blake's worst meaning of that term.

Many of the *Songs* may be seen as visions, and this is a good example. Blake does not attempt to draw an explicit lesson; instead he confronts us with two contrasting images and invites us to use our own imaginations to draw conclusions. But notice also that the rhythms of the poem alter in the last two lines (from **trimeter** to **tetrameter**), providing tangible evidence of the heavy-handedness and ponderousness of the priests and the rules that they work to enforce.

Notice also the important ambiguity of the second line, 'And saw what I never had seen'. The narrator is not necessarily saying that the chapel has suddenly been built in the garden; rather he is saying that *he* had not seen it before. It is open to us therefore to read the poem in two ways. According to the first reading, this gradual encroachment of the world of rules and laws may be a part of the general part of the process of maturation, or indeed of human history. But on the other, it may also be a reflection of the state of mind of the narrator. There would be a state of mind – the 'innocent' state – in which this chapel would have no real existence; but there would also be another state of mind in which it looms large and threatening. This might remind us of a significant possibility about Blake's depiction of the state of experience. He means it, clearly, as a social and historical critique; but he also means to designate by it a psychological state. Perhaps that state is somewhat akin to what we have come much more recently to refer to as depression (Coleridge referred to it as 'dejection'). It is important, though, to remember that this is not to say that Blake believed simply that we interpret the world arbitrarily according to our state of mind; rather he is concerned to explore the connections between particular types of social order and the psychological effects they may have.

CONTEXT

Another relevant term might be 'melancholia', which was a frequent topic among mid eighteenth-century poets; the best example would be William Cowper.

THE LITTLE VAGABOND

- The young street-urchin, although willing to go to church, finds it cold spiritually and physically.
- Only in the ale-house can he find warmth and companionship.

This poem is not, of course, a plea for drunkenness, but rather an appeal for kindness and compassion from a religious and political system that is felt to be 'cold' and unfeeling. More than this, we have also in the last stanza the idea that the very existence of the devil is merely an effect of this lack of feeling, and that a more loving God would be capable of healing all rifts between apparent good and evil.

CHECK THE NET

See if you can follow 'Dame Lurch' through the Net to give you information.

The voice is that of another of Blake's abandoned children; he knows that the ale-house is the only place that will give him shelter, and yet he longs for a better situation, in which the church itself will take up its responsibilities to clothe and feed the poor. 'Dame Lurch' (line 11), an evil folk figure who punishes small children, is regarded by the little vagabond as directly associated with the punitive church as it actually exists; but even she might be redeemed if only the church could relearn the Christian teaching of forgiveness of sins and compassion for the weak.

Yet there seems to be something plaintive, almost hopeless, in the tone of the poem; it is as if the little vagabond can see what the shape of a better life might be like, but this figures for him only as a fantasy, a dream. Perhaps we might even go so far as to see this poem as a delirious, or deathbed scene, in which the protagonist is looking toward a better life but one which, he knows, is never likely really to be manifested in this fallen world of experience.

At the end of the poem, it seems there is a possibility, even if only a fantasised one, that there might be a reconciliation between God and the Devil. This might be taken to refer to the state that Blake calls 'organised innocence'; in other words, a state superior to the partialities of both innocence and experience where these two opposite viewpoints might be harmonised and reconciled. It must be said, though, that Blake rarely depicts this state of bliss: it was obviously clear to him that, if such a state were possible, it did not exist in the England of his day, and it was apparent how it might be achieved. In his longer poems he talks sometimes about the possibility of England, and London in particular, being transformed through the operations of the imagination into a new Jerusalem; but such a vision is here very far away indeed, and the vagabond's hopes seem altogether too improbable for immediate satisfaction. Of course, the thought of God and the devil sitting down to sup together would have seemed to most of Blake's contemporaries – and many Christian people of the present day – to be deeply heretical; it is a mark of Blake's extraordinary ability to think outside accepted categories – today we might call it 'thinking outside the box' – that he is able even to contemplate such a possibility.

LONDON

- The poet walks through the London streets near the River Thames.
- He hears children and chimney sweeps crying, sees blackened churches, hears whores cursing marriage.
- Everywhere is evidence of suffering and unhappiness.

COMMENTARY

The world of innocence is, as we have seen, very frequently a rural world, made up of happy old shepherds and village greens. By contrast the world of experience is composed of what Blake sees around him every day in London: a realm of fragmentary sights and sounds, of man's alienation from his fellows, of 'blights' and 'plagues' (line 16).

It is worth noting also that, although Blake here presents the 'fallen' world of London, elsewhere in his poetry he also presents us with an idea of London redeemed: no location or situation is forever doomed to evil, but salvation will always depend on a change of perspective.

The form of this poem is remarkably tight, even by Blake's standards: notice the repetition of words like 'mark' and 'every',

CHECK THE NET
Try the Blake Digital Text project at http://www.english.uga.edu/~wblake.

and how these words and others chime through the poem, uniting it while at the same time suggesting the repetitive quality of life in the city. There are more questions addressed to this poem in **Extended commentaries – Text 3**; here, however, we might point to the way in which the description of London amounts to a virtual catalogue of the qualities we might associate with experience: 'weakness' and 'woe', the 'cry of fear', the 'blackning' (lines 4, 6 and 10) of the church, the savage insistence on the otherwise hidden relation between the plight of the prostitute and the terrifying 'Marriage hearse' (line 16). In this world, we notice, no real purposes are possible, even for the 'wandering' narrator.

THE HUMAN ABSTRACT

- Fear, cruelty and false humility give rise to the 'Tree of Mystery'.
- This obscures the imagination; but the roots of this tree are to be found in our own minds.

QUESTION
Consider the role of trees in Blake's poems and illustrations.

COMMENTARY

Reversing the terms of 'The Divine Image' in *Songs of Innocence*, this poem spells out with cynical enthusiasm how the authorities have perverted notions of pity and mercy to their ends, and how they use them to justify economic inequality and exploitation. Here all is deceit and hypocrisy, culminating in the 'dismal shade / Of Mystery' (lines 13 and 14), the dreaded tree which occurs often in Blake and is the inversion of the 'tree' (cross) of Christ's crucifixion and serves only to cover over the deadly operations of tyranny.

The sing-along tone here is in direct counterpoint to the violence of the imagery, whereby we are shown how the whole of humanity is perverted by the lies of those in power, of 'God & his Priest & King' (see 'The Chimney-Sweeper'). At the same time, though, the final stanza reminds us, like the 'mind-forg'd manacles' of 'London', that we make a mistake if we look for a solution to our woes in the outside world; these dire things would not occur unless there was something inside us that wills them that way, or at least capitulates in external tyranny.

The title here is all-important: whatever was 'abstract', to Blake, was deathly, it derogated from the fullness of life. For Blake, meaning was not to be found in abstractions or generalisations: these were the work of Urizen, the false creator who rules the world by cutting it up, dividing it, trying to measure it and thus reduce it to fixed categories. Rather, meaning resided in what Blake often called 'minute particulars'.

As in Gerard Manley Hopkins' realm of 'inscape', and Blake's 'minute particulars', there are no external rules: everything is what it is and not another thing, and it is the task of the poet – speaking and writing on behalf of humanity as a whole – to apprehend and articulate this individuality. Notice that in Blake individuality is the opposite of 'selfhood': where selfhood is to do with boundaries, with separating the self off, the apprehension of minute particulars is an act of supreme communication, within which we can thoroughly apprehend the 'soul' of the other.

In contrast to the animals of innocence, and to the grandeur of the 'tyger', we have here 'Catterpiller', 'Fly' and 'Raven' (lines 15 and 19). What do they signify, and how might we link them with the forces of social control? We have here also a transformation of conventionally accepted values: what does it mean to say that 'Humility takes its root' under 'his [cruelty's] foot' (lines 11 and 12), and similarly why should the 'fruit of Deceit' be (or appear to be) 'ruddy and sweet to eat' (lines 17 and 18)?

> **CONTEXT**
>
> You might want to compare Blake's notion of 'minute particulars' with the thoughts of the much later poet Gerard Manley Hopkins. Hopkins speaks of 'inscape', by which he means a process by which we come to apprehend the absolute essence, the 'thingness' of another thing or the central quality, the individuality of a person.

INFANT SORROW

- The baby is born not in joy but in terror.
- It has to become a hypocrite in order to survive the world's dangers.

COMMENTARY

To be read alongside 'Infant Joy', from *Songs of Innocence*, this poem might initially seem more like the *start* of a poem than a finished work. Nonetheless, it gives us a clear picture of what happens to the infant in the world of experience, fearful of the future, oppressed by the role of the father, and finally settling down into a hypocritical sulking.

In Blake's view, the only hope for a child born in such circumstances (and they are, according to him, the prevailing circumstances in the world we ordinarily know) is through the opening of the eyes of the imagination, but here the very foreshortening of the poem prevents any such possibility from being considered. Instead we leave the infant at the point where it has already given up real hope and settled into a malevolent attitude to the world, which we know from Blake's other poems will spring out into open violence as life goes on.

QUESTION
Discuss the roles of childhood in the *Songs of Innocence and of Experience*.

For Blake, the *world* cannot be dangerous, any more than it can be safe; everything depends on how we view it, and so we may say that the child here is merely receiving the perspectives of its parents, from which it has little chance of escaping. Inside the 'cloud' there is a 'fiend' (line 4); forced to hide and suppress its real desires, the child grows up distorted, knowing that it is 'Bound' (line 7) but unable to summon the energy to burst these bonds (or 'bands' – line 6). How, then, are we to take the word 'sorrow' in the title? Who might utter such a word? And, we might add, what is the relation between the two words of the title? More obviously, we might say that this is a poem about the sorrow – or the origins or causes of sorrow – of the infant; but we could equally say that this is a poem about the birth, the infancy of sorrow, and this would be another way of explaining why the poem appears so foreshortened. In the world of experience, it might be impossible to move beyond this position: the world of experience is one in which development had been frozen, and the possibilities of imaginative life have been stifled – if not at birth, then perhaps very shortly afterwards. This we could see as another way of looking at 'abstraction': we foreshorten our own mental and imaginative development when we settle for received interpretations of the way things are. Just as the child here seems unable to progress beyond a limited vision of the world, so all abstract systems, which reduce human individuality, serve to stunt our growth, whether we are thinking here of individuals, particular human societies, or the course of human history as a whole.

A POISON TREE

- The narrator does not confess his anger, and thus it grows more deadly. Like a poison tree, it finally bears fruit.
- His enemy steals into his garden and in the morning is found dead under the tree.

COMMENTARY

This poem is a stark warning against holding grudges: the wrath against the narrator's 'friend' (line 1) is told and is then over and done with, but that which he harbours towards his foe turns into a tree, which bears an apple. The narrator knows that the temptation to steal this apple will be too strong; he knows also that it is poisonous, and thus his revenge is completed – to his own pleasure.

Like the 'tree of mystery', this 'poison tree' is an inversion of the cross, and it is also an inversion of the Tree of Knowledge in the Bible. In the world of experience there can be no genuine knowledge, only the polluted handing on of jealousy and anger which characterises fallen relations between people. In the second stanza, it is as though 'fears', 'tears', 'smiles' and 'wiles' (lines 5, 6, 7, 8) have all become the same: in this realm of hypocrisy and disguise there is no longer any way to distinguish between different emotions, for all are at the service of the lust for vengeance.

This image is one of Blake's most intricate, although closely related to the tree in 'The Human Abstract'. Its complexity is partly caused by the fact that in the world of experience it is difficult to apportion blame, for we are all afflicted, or infected, by the same perversions of human value. Thus we may here criticise the narrator; but to what extent do we have to involve the 'foe' (line 3) too, since he succumbs to the temptation to steal the apple – or is he merely an innocent victim of the machinations of the protagonist?

This is a particularly eloquent example of the ways in which Blake takes up key elements in Christian imagery and develops them for his own ends. The apple is, obviously, the apple that causes the downfall of Adam and Eve in the Garden of Eden; but here the

CONTEXT

The Fall is the work of the Devil, but also the work of the serpent; thus referring back to the 'worm' in 'The Sick Rose'.

narrative position is all-important. For the temptation that was offered to Adam and Eve was, we are told in the Bible, the work of the devil; here it seems to be the work of the narrator. This is crucial, since it places the narrator precisely in the position of the devil. We may therefore say that in the realm of experience each of us finds ourselves enacting diabolic plans and plots: it is a world of paranoia and vengeance, and, even worse, a world in which we feel pleasure when our destructive plots are successful. Thus the 'position of the Devil' becomes something that we all succumb to in the world of experience: we may have knowledge of our own motives – greater knowledge, perhaps, than is available in the world of innocence - but we do not use this knowledge to improve our relations to other people, rather we use it for destructive ends, acting under the delusion that the diminution or harm of other people in some way helps us whereas, in fact, we are all diminished and damaged by the damage we cause to others.

A LITTLE BOY LOST

- A little boy dares to question the institutional wisdom of a priest.
- As a terrible punishment he is burned to death.

COMMENTARY

Here the innocent questions of the little boy are enough to excite the wrath of the tyrannous priest, who thinks he hears blasphemy in the boy's words because he does not understand the (in truth, unintelligible) 'Mystery' (line 16) which the priest claims to guard. The boy thus becomes a sacrifice, one of many offered up to the cruel god Urizen.

CHECK THE BOOK
Read Blake's poem *The First Book of Urizon* for further insight.

This boy is clearly not 'lost' in the sense of the wandering children of other *Songs*; he is instead 'lost' to the lies of conventional religion, and as a result he is truly 'lost' in death. Yet even this is not enough for Blake, who insists that 'all admir'd the Priestly care' (line 12) as we have now seen often before, cruelty is excused when it goes under the false banner of holiness, and even the boy's own and his parents' protests have no effect on the nameless 'They' (line 19) the unenlightened crowd led by priests, who regard it as their duty to enforce the moral law.

And yet, what after all is it that the boy is saying in the first two stanzas? At first glance it might seem as though he is uttering a kind of selfishness (like that of the 'Pebble' in 'The Clod & the Pebble'); but would this make sense in terms of the rest of the poem, or should we rather think that he is simply speaking an innocent, unthought truth, brought out by his likening himself to the 'little bird' (line 7)? On this reading, he would simply be offering the priest what love he has, but this seems not to be enough. Why is it not enough? What more, or what else, does the priest want?

? QUESTION
In what ways is loss a critical theme in the *Songs*?

What he wants, one might say, is mystery, hiddenness, a sense that only he is privy to the truth. This has directly theological ramifications, in terms of the Christian conflict between the notion of a Catholic church that asserts the authority of the priesthood and the reforming tendencies of Protestantism which asserts, on the contrary, the possibility of the immediate contact of the individual with God irrespective of priestly intercession. However, Blake's point goes far beyond this: the boy is simply stating what is, in a sense, obvious, namely that one can only love according to one's experience; all else is abstraction. But to the priest this means that he is contravening some higher law of which he, the priest, is custodian; and therefore it is important to 'make an example' of this boy, who is speaking without due authority. Perhaps if one were to wish to summarise Blake's position on theological disputes, one could do no better than to begin from this phrase, 'speaking without due authority'; Blake thought that we all have a right to speak, however young or old, or from whatever perspective, and that it was our duty as well as our joy to find the sources of our speech – our inspiration – inside ourselves. For Blake, this was clearly a view that he thought the established church – or other established authorities – could not bear; and it would seem at least arguable that history has many times proved him right.

A LITTLE GIRL LOST

- Two lovers revel in an Edenic setting.
- But when the girl approaches her father her joy gives way to fear.

? QUESTION
How similar does Blake's view of Eden seem to be to the view given in the Bible?

This poem starts, unusually, with Blake's own interpretation: the poem, he says, recounts the criminalising of love and desire. The scene, of course, is Adam and Eve in the Garden of Eden, although Blake clearly means them to **symbolise** the situation of all young lovers who come to suffer the repression of the moral law; the first four stanzas recount an idyllic scenario of mutual and fulfilled desire, but all is ruined when the 'maiden' (line 7) comes to her father.

Quite how this ruin occurs is perhaps not clear: we are told that the father's look is 'loving' (line 27), but since it is then related to the 'holy book' (line 28) we may surmise that this is the wrong kind of love, which is why the maiden is terrified, and her fears seem to be justified by his words, in which he pronounces himself as fearful as she is of what she will reveal. Although he may well believe himself to be a caring, loving father, it is obvious to his daughter, and to the reader, that he intends to sit in judgement over her rather than accepting her freedom, and to this extent is incapable of imaginative sympathy with her situation.

It is interesting, in line 24, that Blake refers to the lovers as 'tired wanderers'. We have now encountered these images of 'straying', 'wandering' and being lost many times in the Songs, and sometimes with quite different connotations. But they do always, it would seem fair to say, signify moments when people move beyond the constraints of what I have referred to above as the 'moral law'; in other words, moments when people have found ways of escape from constraint. Here the implications are particularly clear, in the opposition between that law and the possibility of sexual freedom. But the notion of 'wandering' also, in its positive sense, represents for Blake a more general feeling of being free – or making oneself sufficiently free – to move around the world in ways that contravene conventional boundaries. Blake himself was perhaps not a 'wanderer' in a geographical sense; but although he would no doubt have said that it is imaginative wandering that is the crucial thing, nonetheless the *Songs* do conjure up a strong sense that the more ordinary sense of wandering – of not being confined by the rules of place, location, city – is also important.

Blake addresses this poem to the future; this suggests that he believes his own age to be too much under the rule of constrictive law to be able fully to hear his words, and it also suggests one of the senses in which we might construe Blake's frequent use of the term 'prophetic'. Blake also refers to his *'page'* (poem) as *'indignant'* (line 2) does this strike you as appropriate, or would we use a different term nowadays?

TO TIRZAH

- Humans are all born ultimately to die.
- The protagonist, addressing the figure of Tirzah, who represents sexuality and reproduction, announces that he has been freed from her control by Jesus.

COMMENTARY

In the first stanza, he says that mortal life implies death, while at the same time asserting the necessity of rising 'free' from the world of 'Generation' (physical reproduction). To do so must require that he renounce all his ties with the material world, and in the third stanza he goes on to accuse his mother of deliberate cruelty and violence towards him. He claims that she has specifically 'bound' or restricted the development of his senses, and has thus condemned him to merely mortal life, whereas the Christian message comes to remind us that there is another life beyond mortality.

 CHECK THE BOOK

On 'Generation', 'Beulah' and other 'states', check Northrop Frye's *Fearful Symmetry* (see **Further reading**).

The most important issue in this poem concerns the protagonist's attitude. There is no reason to doubt his sincerity when he speaks of the 'Death of Jesus' (line 15) or when he twice asks the question Jesus himself asked of his own mortal mother. But biblical commentators have seen that question itself as remarkably cruel; and we have to ask whether the argument apparently advocated is not in fact too extreme, too exaggerated to win Blake's authorial approval. Perhaps the protagonist is seeking for an imaginative transcendence of the material world; but can it be right to seek this at the expense of all emotional ties and responsibilities? Similarly, do we necessarily believe the narrator in his condemnation of his mother, or might we think him singularly lacking in compassion and thus a figure representing at least an admixture of experience into imaginative truth? Or in making these 'liberal' suggestions, are we in fact understating the true radicalism of Blake?

THE SCHOOL-BOY

- Outside on a summer morning all nature is joyful.
- A school boy, caged in his classroom, misses the freedom of the natural world outside.

COMMENTARY

The school boy is having a terrible time; he remembers what it is like to 'rise in a summer morn' (line 1) without constraint, but this memory combines with all his present experience of school, of rule and regulation, only to make him the more miserable and the more certain that he is wasting the all too brief spring and summer of his life.

 CHECK THE NET

Look up 'Wordsworth and childhood' on the Net.

These beautifully formed stanzas may be seen as constituting an appeal, from the heart, against the early imposition of unnecessary, unnatural learning. Rather like Wordsworth, Blake sees formal education not as an advantage but rather as all too often a damming up of the soul's creative spirit; to be at school is to be taken away from the more real education that can be provided by roaming the mountains and the streams. Lines like 14 and 15 ('Nor sit in learnings bower, / Worn thro' with the dreary shower') brilliantly develop the crucial **metaphors** of the poem: this 'shower' is not the refreshing, rejuvenating 'spring shower' that the growing boy should be experiencing but rather the dull drizzle of unexplained work.

The poem appears to express a viewpoint of disillusion that one might naturally associate with the scepticism or cynicism of the *Songs of Experience* although it originally appeared in the *Songs of*

Innocence. It continues, however, to express the child's view, no matter how embittered he might be becoming under the impact of rote learning and an education that only amounts to induction, a 'leading in' or training in the presumed necessities of life rather than a 'leading out' towards real understanding and freedom.

It is important here to register the proper force of the thirteenth line: 'Nor in my book can I take delight' (line 13). It is not that Blake is saying that 'books' are somehow of themselves dry and discouraging; it is that the circumstances under which the schoolboy is required to read his book, the imposition of controls and constraints on his reading and learning, are damaging. Later Blake was to develop his ideas on the function of 'the book' in complex ways. Obviously, as a writer, and more so as a maker of books that contained both visual and verbal work, he was committed to the importance of the book as such. Equally, his unusual methods for publishing his work meant that he was essentially at odds with conventional techniques of reproducing and publishing. In the Prophetic Books, he writes at considerable length about Urizen's books, which are always conceived of as made of metal, as heavy, dense tomes that repel the reader even while they seek to aspire to a false scientific exactitude. But there is no doubt that in Blake's mind there other kinds of book, liberating books, just as there are kinds of writing – and of singing, and of piping – that serve a liberating function: as always, all is in the context in which these books are encountered.

> **CONTEXT**
>
> For Blake on the book, the crucial context remains the Bible, and the beginning of St John's Gospel: 'In the beginning was the Word'.

THE VOICE OF THE ANCIENT BARD

- The 'voice' calls the 'youth of delight' to arise and greet a new morning.
- But the voice also notes the ravages of false reason.

COMMENTARY

This poem is another one that Blake transferred between the *Songs of Innocence* and the *Songs of Experience*, and it is easy to see why: although it speaks of the 'Youth of delight' (line 1) it also becomes increasingly embroiled in the problems of false reason which were to concern Blake for the whole of his life. Reason here figures as an unwelcome, indeed disastrous, involvement with the past and its rules and traditions; and it is scarcely obvious that this 'youth', whoever or whatever it is, can escape the 'entanglement' which awaits him.

QUESTION
In *Songs of Experience*, do either age or experience produce wisdom?

Here we have Blake speaking with a kind of immediacy again, as at the beginning of the *Songs of Innocence*, but with a vastly different voice. It is as though he speaks from the grave; speaks with a voice from which all innocence has gone, and thus he comments also, enigmatically, on the *Songs of Experience* which have followed.

The imagery here is crucial to an understanding of the notion of experience and its relation to innocence. Consider certain key phrases: 'clouds of reason', 'Dark disputes & artful teazing', the 'endless maze', the 'Tangled roots' (lines 4, 5, 6 and 7). All these are for Blake means by which we may be trapped by thinking too much, because *thinking* for Blake, at least in its conventional formulations, does not aim towards truth, rather it separates us from truth, because truth is known not by reason but by the imagination, not by complexity but by residing in our memories of simplicity and in what these memories might permit us to create.

A DIVINE IMAGE

- Even such destructive aspects as cruelty, jealousy, terror and secrecy cannot be separated from our common humanity.

This poem was replaced in *Songs of Experience* by 'The Human Abstract', but it still seems valuable to comment on it here. The first stanza summarises the perverted version of humanity which obtains in the world of experience, while the second constructs a violent, metallic, sealed version of humanity which also plays on the image of the forge which we have come across before in, for example, 'The Tyger'.

Notice the extremely careful way this poem is constructed, with the 'Heart', 'Face', 'Form' and 'Dress' (in the first stanza) referred to again in the opposite order in the second stanza. What is perhaps most important throughout is the use of the word 'Human'; Blake clearly does not mean it here in the approving sense in which he constantly refers to the real, imaginative world as human-shaped; rather, he means to draw attention to how such thoughts, and perhaps more particularly such words, can be appropriated and changed by those in power; this, to Blake, was true blasphemy.

The poem also contains a mention of the 'Human Form Divine' (line 3). Although he is using it here in a debased form, the phrase was of crucial importance to him, signifying that the world as we should see it is in the shape of the human, and that there is no difference or severance between the human and the divine, despite the efforts of priests to maintain a religion of 'mystery'. To liken the human form to a 'fiery Forge' (line 6), however, carries a range of meanings. What might they be?

CHECK THE BOOK

On blasphemy in Blake's time, look at Jon Mee, *Dangerous Enthusiasm* (see **Further reading**).

EXTENDED COMMENTARIES

TEXT 1 – THE CHIMNEY SWEEPER (FROM SONGS OF INNOCENCE)

When my mother died I was very young,
And my father sold me while yet my tongue,
Could scarcely cry weep weep weep weep.
So your chimneys I sweep & in soot I sleep.

Theres little Tom Dacre, who cried when his head
That curl'd like a lambs back, was shav'd, so I said,
Hush Tom never mind it, for when your head's bare,
You know that the soot cannot spoil your white hair.

And so he was quiet, & that very night,
As Tom was a sleeping he had such a sight,
That thousands of sweepers Dick, Joe, Ned & Jack
Were all of them lock'd up in coffins of black,

And by came an Angel who had a bright key,
And he open'd the coffins & set them all free.
Then down a green plain leaping laughing they run
And wash in a river and shine in the Sun.

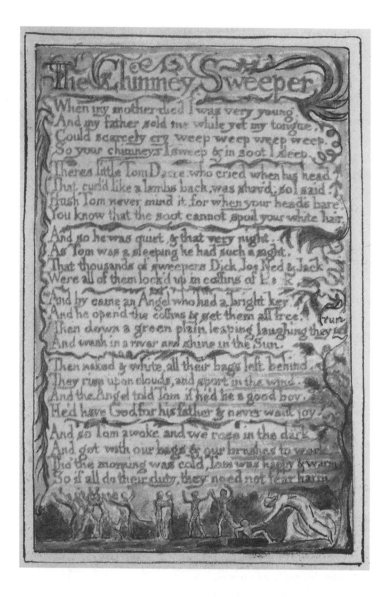

Then naked & white, all their bags left behind,
They rise upon clouds, and sport in the wind.
And the Angel told Tom, if he'd be a good boy,
He'd have God for his father & never want joy.

And so Tom awoke and we rose in the dark
And got with our bags & our brushes to work.
Tho' the morning was cold, Tom was happy & warm.
So if all do their duty, they need not fear harm.

I have chosen this poem to look at in some detail because it
confronts us immediately with a problem concerning the nature of
innocence as Blake saw it. The setting of the poem is one resonant
with echoes from the late eighteenth century. At that time young
children were used as chimney sweepers because only they could
climb up the narrow chimneys which needed cleaning; such was the
poverty of many families in the cities, in London in particular, that
children would be effectively sold as slaves to the sweeps. We know
much more about their plight as a result of recent research; for
example, we know that their life expectation was low and many
who survived were permanently crippled as a result of the work
and of the poor food which was all they could afford to eat.

CHECK THE BOOK

For a later comparison, read one of Charles Dicken's novels of childhood, e.g. *Oliver Twist*.

Blake here presents us with this scene; but the problem with the
poem is to discern where the narrator is, and what we, as readers,
are meant to think about the situation. To put it another way,
clearly we as readers are here 'addressed' or, as some critics would
say, **interpellated** by the poem; but what is to be our response?

One response which seems unavoidable is of pity; we pity the child
for the back-breaking work he does. But what do we think of his
(the child/narrator's) advice to his colleague Tom Dacre? Are we
supposed to think it true that if we all simply get on and do what
we are told to do, then all will be right with the world? Or,
conversely, does the poem say to us that, although the narrator may
believe this to be the case, nonetheless we as readers and as citizens
must be forced to see through this ideology of repression and see
the narrator as a 'victim of innocence' who needs to be enlightened
by seeing issues of exploitation in their full guise?

These are certainly important questions; perhaps equally important is that Blake does not answer them for us. Instead, he deliberately poses his poem in the form of a question: is innocence a valuable perspective on the world, or is it instead at the service of manipulation and greed? And he leads us further into these complexities through his recounting of Tom's dream. For what is this dream supposed to imply? Are we to think that a naïve, simple religious belief can compensate us for suffering? Are we meant to think that, if we merely change our attitudes, we can come to enjoy even the most loathsome aspects of our lot? Or are we meant to see, with a certain **irony**, the ways in which religion colludes with other forms of tyranny in offering us false pleasures which merely serve to ensure that we do not challenge our masters?

QUESTION
Does Blake appear to believe that paradise on earth is truly possible?

To take the question one step further, we might think about the presence of death in the poem. The scene presented by the dream is quite obviously redolent of Paradise; the question becomes one of when, where and how we shall find this Paradise, and at least three answers are possible. One is that we can find it by looking at the present world through transformed eyes; a second is that it does not exist at all, and we find it only by closing our eyes to reality and retiring within our own imagination; and the third is that we can find it indeed, but only on the other side of death. This third view would then persuade us that Tom himself, and the narrator too, are deluded by the dream; the only time when we may 'shine in the Sun' (line 16) will be when we have died, by which time it will, as always, be too late for change.

And if this is so, then we may also surmise that Blake is saying that the exercise of innocence may all too rapidly conduce to this death; if we persist in not understanding the facts of experience, however damaging and wearying they may seem, then we shall continue to submit to the most appalling of practices, content – because God has told us to be – in our hopes of an immaculate future, literally 'out of this world'.

Our **interpretation** of the poem will also, of course, have to take into account other factors, such as the **symbolic** role of 'black' and 'white'; and we also need to consider carefully the role of the 'Angel' (line 13). In Blake's work, angels are very often bad news;

that is to say, they stand for the kind of person who believes unquestioningly that right is on their side. Whereas devils enact the rule of energy and the imagination, angels stand for a kind of purity, for reason, for everything that puts a brake on energy and prevents it from bursting out.

It is perhaps important at this point to go to another work of Blake's, *The Marriage of Heaven and Hell*. In this work, which is a mixture of prose and poetry, Blake also presents the reader with a series of 'proverbs', which he titles 'The Proverbs of Hell'. Some of the best known (and most relevant to Blake's understanding of devils and angels) are as follows:

'The road of excess leads to the palace of wisdom'
(plate 7, line 3)

'He who desires but acts not, breeds pestilence'
(plate 7, line 5)

'The tygers of wrath are wiser than the horses of instruction'
(plate 9, line 5)

'Exuberance is beauty'   (plate 10, line 4).

There are many possible interpretations of these proverbs, but the important point about them is precisely that they are the proverbs of 'Hell'; in other words, they are 'contraries' to established Christian wisdom. Whereas, in Blake's view, Christianity tended to place its highest valuations on submissive and conventional behaviour, the religion he sought was one full of fire, enthusiasm and energy, one which would allow every person – perhaps even every creature – to develop his or her full individuality untrammelled by the power of the State or by the restrictions of reason. This kind of development was something which, for Blake, the 'Angels' would never allow, and in his search for an alternative he sometimes went to lengths which might now seem to us quite strange – as in, for example, the most notorious of the proverbs of Hell, 'Sooner murder an infant in its cradle than nurse unacted desires' (plate 10, line 7). Blake is not, of course, saying that it is all right to murder babies; but he is saying that if we seek to restrain

CHECK THE BOOK

Read Blake's *The Marriage of Heaven and Hell.* See *Blake: Complete Writings,* edited by Geoffrey Keyne, Oxford University Press, 1966, p. 146.

and control our desires too forcefully, if we allow them no outlet, then it may well be that those desires will turn poisonous or, indeed, murderous.

CHECK THE BOOK
Read about Blake's symbolism in S. Foster Damon's *A Blake Dictionary* (see **Further reading**).

Thus we may read the poem as an account of those forces that prevent people from an essential and liberating rebellion. Tom is obviously sad at the beginning, but then he is cheered up by this – probably false – account of the rewards that will be his. What, then, does this make of the narrator? One thing we can say clearly, which is that the narrator is not innocent, he is at some level aware of the deceptions that form the heart of the poem. And thus we have here a song *of* innocence, but not in the sense of a song from an innocent standpoint, rather a song which is *about* innocence, and is thus enabled to present its consolations without subscribing to them.

I would invite you to address several questions about this poem. In the first stanza it refers to '*your* chimneys'; what is the force of this? Stanza 2 compares Tom's hair to a 'lambs back'; what might the significance of this be, in general and in terms of the other *Songs*? I mentioned above that this poem might be in some sense about death; how, then, might one see the 'coffins' of stanza 3, and how might they relate to the chimneys, and to the general issue of fire and smoke? In stanza 4, might we speculate about what this 'key' is that the Angel has? In stanza 5, the word 'want' might attract our interest; it bears two meanings, and this was conventional at the time the poem was written, but even so we might want to ask ourselves: what is the difference between its two meanings, 'desire' and 'lack'? And finally, the last line of the poem seems to have the form of a proverb; what might we think about the role of proverbs in the *Songs* and in Blake's work generally?

TEXT 2 – THE TYGER (FROM SONGS OF EXPERIENCE)

Tyger Tyger, burning bright,
In the forests of the night;
What immortal hand or eye,
Could frame thy fearful symmetry?

In what distant deeps or skies,
Burnt the fire of thine eyes?
On what wings dare he aspire?
What the hand, dare sieze the fire?

And what shoulder, & what art,
Could twist the sinews of thy heart?
And when thy heart began to beat,
What dread hand? & what dread feet?

What the hammer? what the chain,
In what furnace was thy brain?
What the anvil? what dread grasp,
Dare its deadly terrors clasp?

When the stars threw down their spears
And water'd heaven with their tears:
Did he smile his work to see?
Did he who made the Lamb make thee?

Tyger Tyger burning bright,
In the forests of the night:
What immortal hand or eye,
Dare frame thy fearful symmetry?

CHECK THE NET

Start looking at the history of big cats in captivity at http://lynx.vio.no/catfolk.

Perhaps Blake's best-known poem, 'The Tyger' is ruled by symmetry: symmetry between stanzas, between lines, and within lines. Yet, for this very reason, one of the details which leaps immediately to our attention is the lack of symmetry between the first and last stanzas, where a single word – 'could' – in stanza 1 is changed to 'dare' in stanza 6. To confront this change is immediately to ask crucial questions of the poem, and indeed of the

tyger; for what in the poem has led us to regard the tyger under an aspect which makes us 'dare' to approach it?

The answer, of course, is that the tyger has been portrayed, in a curious term, as a 'dread' beast (line 12) – 'dread' in English is one of those rare words that can mean its own opposite, both 'fearsome' and 'fearing'. So the question immediately follows: what is being feared here by whom, and why? Or, to put it another way, what does this tyger represent, and thus, what might it mean to try to 'frame' the tyger's 'fearful symmetry' (line 24)?

The poem suggests two answers, and in doing so proposes a whole theory of the human and the divine. For on one interpretation, of course, the tyger, like all other beasts and like man himself, has been 'framed' – in the sense of made – by God, and the poem does not deny this, even though it refuses to name the answer to the question. But on another **interpretation**, the responsibility for 'framing' the tyger – in the sense now of converting him into a work of art – rests not with God but with the artist, the poet; and therefore we may see Blake's poem as asking a reflexive question about the role of the writer, and about the writer's – and artist's – relation with the 'untameable' materials of the imagination with which he works.

What might these untameable materials be? Well, they clearly might simply be the 'wild' itself – wild nature, the beast 'out there'. But they might equally well – and as well – refer to the wild inside, the 'beast within'; the unconscious within us all, that compound of desires and drives which always and everywhere rises up to upset the attempted rule of 'framing' reason. Thus the tyger stands as an emblem for energy, for a power which, while in one important sense 'symmetrical' – that is to say, perfectly formed – is also beyond all framing, control, capture.

CHECK THE BOOK
Read about Blake's visual art in Mitchell's *Blake's Composite Art* (see **Further reading**).

The fires with which the tyger burns are thus both the fires of that which is unapproachable, unassailable, that which is forever hidden in the 'forests of the night' (line 2) – its stripes blending perfectly with its jungle backdrop – and at the same time the fires of the creative soul, burning with the desire to 'frame' – create – an image. This image, the poem appears to tell us, cannot in the end fully be made: there is no real possibility of 'capturing' the tyger, with pen or with paint. And yet, and paradoxically at the same time, the very act of naming the impossibility of capturing the tyger actually captures it; so that in this poem, as in the accompanying illustration, we do indeed, and despite everything, 'see' the tyger. And we hear it too. The dull, threatening stamp of the lines, the repetition of '**dread**', these are precisely the incarnation of the tyger's walk out from the jungle to meet us, the irrepressibility of the tyger within us all, and at the same time the terror of the artist confronted with the internal nature which he tries at the same time to suppress and to represent.

And this brings us to what many critics have considered to be the crux of the poem, which occurs in the fifth stanza. When the stars '**threw down their spears / And water'd heaven with their tears**' (lines 17–18) in what mood are they doing that? Are they throwing down their spears in the sense of attempting to ambush their mighty earth-bound opponent? Or are they 'throwing down their spears' in the sense we might use today of 'throwing in the towel', abandoning all hope of divine, angelic supremacy in the face of a power which, while perhaps uncomprehending of its own strength, is nonetheless far more mighty than they? Who is really in charge here, the 'stars' or the tyger?

And, by the same token, we might ask: who is in charge in the writing of a poem, the painting of a picture, the human being who attempts to 'capture' the world outside with pen or brush, or the wild material itself which will continually outpace any attempt to render reality in artistic or textual form? And, we may go on to ask, who gets to 'smile' at this process?

Perhaps God smiles; or perhaps he does not, when he compares his work of making the tyger with the gentler work of making the lamb. Or perhaps he does indeed smile upon the tyger (we may know of other references to 'the smile on the face of the tyger') but only with a smile of **irony**, because he sees in the tyger precisely the equivalent of a force of destruction.

Is the tyger, we might also ask, a natural or an unnatural beast? Natural, of course: for tigers are real, they do exist, and they resist

CONTEXT
Yet the illustration of the 'tyger' is surprisingly mild – it is worth wondering whether this is deliberate.

all attempts to tame them. But here, the tyger is unreal too: he is a *made* beast, and made in a quite specific way, made with, for example, hammer, chain and anvil, made with all the apparatus of human making; and thus some critics have been led to see in the tyger a figure for a monster, a specific monster constructed from bits and pieces, an emblem for the industrial revolution, and for the kind of making which man might indeed achieve but which might swiftly move out of control, if indeed it is not out of control already.

CONTEXT

Frankenstein was written by Mary Shelley not long afterwards (in 1818).

And this issue of 'monstrosity', of the making of monsters, while it may not feature particularly significantly in the *Songs*, was to become a major motif in his later work, in which he becomes more and more concerned with different kinds of human work and with the importance of distinguishing between those kinds of work or labour which allow for individuality and creativity and those other kinds – increasingly prevalent as industrialisation develops – which are – for Blake, quite literally – 'soul-destroying'. The Prophetic Books are full of characters labouring over machines, working in dehumanising and dehumanised conditions; we might think of them almost as zombies, bodies without souls, slaves of the machine. Over against these characters frequently stands a mythical figure of Blake's own invention, known as Los. Los stands for a quite different kind of work, the work of the imagination; it is his constant attempt to rehumanise work and thus to defeat the destructive forces of Urizen, although his own name perhaps suggests the uncertainty of this struggle and the possibility of 'loss' that it entails. It needs to be said too that this opposition in Blake has a bearing on his attitude to his own creative work. Whether he invents his mythology of creativity in response to his own disappointment at not gaining a wide audience in his day, or whether he deliberately sets out to work in so personalised a way as to make mass production of his texts impossible, the fact remains that his way of writing and the characteristics of his visual art place him very far indeed from the norms of his age, and engage him constantly in a very different kind of work from his artistic and literary peers.

A final question. In one copy of the poem Blake altered line 12 from 'What dread hand? & what dread feet?' to 'What dread hand

CHECK THE NET

Look up Blake's art on the net. What, if anything, does it add to his poetry?

form'd thy dread feet?' – what effect does this change have on the poem? What effect does it have on our ideas of the 'stability' of any poem? Do we believe that individual poems are laid down for all time, or can they be altered, as Blake was continually altering much of his own work? This is one of the many questions with which Blake confronts us, and it is relevant to the overall theme of 'The Tyger', which, we might think, is all about stability and instability, reason and energy, that which will always exceed our attempt to 'frame' a reasonable explanation of life.

TEXT 3 – LONDON
(FROM SONGS OF EXPERIENCE)

I wander thro' each charter'd street,
Near where the charter'd Thames does flow
And mark in every face I meet
Marks of weakness, marks of woe.

In every cry of every Man,
In every Infants cry of fear,
In every voice; in every ban,
The mind-forg'd manacles I hear

How the Chimney-sweepers cry
Every blackning Church appalls,
And the hapless Soldiers sigh
Runs in blood down Palace walls

But most thro' midnight streets I hear
How the youthful Harlots curse
Blasts the new-born Infants tear
And blights with plagues the Marriage hearse

'London' is probably the most concisely violent assault on 'establishment' thinking English poetry has yet produced; but an understanding of the power of this attack can only be securely based on an appreciation of the remarkable **rhetorical** qualities of the poem. Consider, for example, the function of that simplest and most basic of all rhetorical devices, repetition: the repetition of 'every', which hammers through the poem like the dull boot of totalitarianism; the repetition of 'charter'd' which brings within itself two virtually opposing meanings, 'charter'd' as 'freed' and 'charter'd' as 'constrained'; the repetition in two different stanzas of the 'Infants', which emphasises in the first instance the child's terror and bewilderment at the world in which it finds itself, and in the second establishes with frightening force the source of this bewilderment in the confusion of love and sex, life and death, which, for Blake, characterises the world in which he finds himself.

 CHECK THE BOOK

John Mee's *Dangerous Enthusiasm: William Blake and the Culture of Radicalism in the 1790*, provides some really useful contexts (see **Further reading**).

It needs also to be remarked that this is a poem which is remarkable for its auditory and visual power. To take the issue of hearing first: we have here cries, voices and 'bans' – these latter again in a double sense, bans as prohibitions, and banns as the words read out in Church to permit marriage. All of these sounds relate to the general scenario of the poem, to the poet's everyday walk through the streets of London, to the 'comminglings' of sounds he hears in this puzzling, multi-layered city in which nothing is as it seems, in which everything is estranged from its inner sources.

> **? QUESTION**
> How much of London did Blake know? (See Ackroyd in **Further reading**).

Yet it is almost as if the narrator were free from the power of hearing, for his work is also the work of seeing: he sees – and 'Marks' (line 4), in the doubled sense of 'noticing' or 'remarking upon' and of 'marking down on paper' – these faces, and he sees also a terrible vision, which is of the churches dripping with darkness, the palaces soaked in blood. Where ordinary men might have seen these bastions of the mighty and the safe as essential and quasi-natural features of the cityscape, Blake immediately connects them back to the sources of their grandeur; to the poor and the suffering, to the 'Soldiers' and the 'Harlots' (lines 11 and 14) who are emblematic victims of the fate of those who live in cities and are cut off from a more natural life, but more importantly wilfully severed from the imaginative vision which alone could provide them with a full understanding of their surroundings. Rich and powerful men do not fight their own battles.

This is a poem, then, which deals in opposites brought together: perhaps the most outstanding example occurs in the final lines, where 'Blasts the new-born Infants tear' (line 15) is coupled with 'blights with plagues the Marriage hearse' (line 16). What is Blake indicting here? Is it merely the practice of whoredom, for example, or is he bringing into breathtakingly close conjunction the stifling nature of conventional marriage, as he saw it, and the victimisation which attends the lot of the harlot? What 'plagues' does he mean, the purely emotional plagues of those who are not happy with their lot, or the more conspicuous and socially problematic plagues of venereal disease? And to take the other crucial example of an extended complex image in the poem, what are we to make of the notion that 'the Chimney-sweepers cry / Every blackning Church appalls' (lines 9–10)? If we were to take 'appall' in its late twentieth-century usage, we would suggest that the church is – or should be – appalled, indeed scandalised, by these brute facts of poverty and child cruelty; but if we look at 'appalls' instead in the sense that that which is 'appalled' is, more literally, covered in a dark shroud, then we could hypothesise that Blake also thinks that the pretensions to purity which the church vaunts are themselves sullied, reduced to blackness, by the brutality of which it chooses to remain unaware.

What lies behind this poem is a terrible indictment – of injustice, certainly, but also of lack of imagination. What Blake is saying is that it is all too easy to remain unaware of the connections between things; to accuse the soldier, for example, of warmongering without remembering that he is probably a soldier in the first place because of the deprived circumstances of his upbringing (why else would one want to be a soldier?) and that his tears too, tears of pain, resentment, repentance and anger, are conjured by those who still lie snugly within their palaces, no matter who fights for or against them, no matter how many get slaughtered, no matter how many 'rivers of blood' may flow in order to secure their safe position.

Blake is famous for his rejection of the notion of 'system', a concept he associates with rationalism and the dreaded unholy trinity of Bacon, Newton and Locke, thinkers whose work he vociferously rejected on the grounds of its reliance on reason, science and the moral law. Nevertheless, it is worth noticing here and elsewhere what an acute eye he actually had for particular kinds of system, for the hidden connections that held together the emerging phenomena of the city. Blake himself would have referred to this as seeing things with 'fourfold vision' – seeing things in all their interrelations, in their total context – and it seems to have been something that he did instinctively, refusing to compartmentalise but constantly asserting that everything is connected together, the pains and perils of everyday life cannot be simply separated from humanity's higher aspirations and desires, the poverty of the many cannot be cut off from the prosperity of the few.

It is important in this poem that the narrator 'wanders': he does not set out upon some purposive activity; were we, for example, to set out to discover instances of injustice, why then, we would immediately see whatever we needed in order to justify our preconceptions. But this narrator claims to have no preconceptions: he claims merely to set out into the streets of London to observe what may be observed; and what he observes is horrific; it is, he says, the product of 'mind-forg'd manacles' (line 8). How are we to interpret this vexed phrase, which has been the subject of prolonged debate? One interpretation would have it that we are all the subjects of manacles, handcuffs, restraints, forged by other minds: in other words, we are all victims of others' ideologies. Another view would say that the real problem is that these manacles are forged by ourselves; in other words, we appear willingly to succumb to the restraints placed upon us and to become victims of our own exploitation. Between, or around, these two interpretations, there is the ambiguity which runs through and through Blake's work: does 'forg'd' mean 'shaped through heating and hammering', or does it mean 'counterfeit'? If it is counterfeit, then all we need to do to realise our freedom is to rise up and throw off these fake manacles, which have never been 'authentic' in the first place; but at the same time, insofar as 'forg'd' means also shaped through great effort, then our attempts to break them in the name of a wider vision will always be thwarted, we shall prove too weak to emerge from the chains of ideas which have been thrown around our wrists and necks by those in power.

> **CONTEXT**
>
> Many of the years of Blake's life were years of violent restraint by the government.

Which of these **interpretations** do you believe most likely, and how can you justify that reading? Or do you believe that Blake deliberately chose to leave this crucial point unresolved, and if so why? Or perhaps it is that a poem, like any text, has its own force: perhaps the jamming together of images which official accounts of social life keep apart – marriage and syphilis, for example – serves its own purpose, and does not need to be translated into more practical action, even if the limits of the language permitted theoretical resolution. Or perhaps Blake was really despairing: saying, for example, that the operation of these repressive systems of thought is so strong that there is no escape. In 'London', is there any escape? And what would such an escape mean, and where might it lead us?

PART THREE

CRITICAL APPROACHES

THEMES

INNOCENCE AND EXPERIENCE

What are the *Songs of Innocence and of Experience* about? Well, the most obvious answer is that they are about what they say they are about, the two 'contrary states' of 'Innocence' and 'Experience', and that the individual poems in the two books are exemplars of these states. Innocence, then, would be, as we have seen, the condition essentially allied to childhood: a condition in which we can view the natural and human world without fear, and can feel confident that we have a home in that world. Behind this, of course, lies a whole realm of biblical myth, in particular the Garden of Eden, although there are significant differences between the biblical Garden and Blakean innocence.

Perhaps the most obvious difference concerns sexuality. Adam and Eve, after all, were ejected from the Garden because of their accession to carnal knowledge, and throughout Christianity there is a connection between sex and the fall of man. To Blake things were quite otherwise: the world of innocence is one of natural, unforced pleasure in sexuality, as in all other things of the body, and it is interesting that this significant alteration of emphasis constitutes one of Blake's many prefigurations of the much later discoveries of Freud, who first demonstrated systematically the sexual interests of the infant.

Innocence, however, cannot last forever unchallenged, although it is always possible to prolong or regain it temporarily: through love, through poetry, through beauty. It is, however, inevitably under threat of being superseded as we move into adulthood and encounter cares, duties, responsibilities. But – and this is a very important point to Blake – although this 'progression' – which is also a fall from grace – is inevitable, it is *also* true that we make it much worse than it needs to be. We make it worse through all kinds of tyranny and harshness at the political level; through the rule of the moral law and an ethic of punishment rather than

CHECK THE BOOK

Some of the best essays on Blake can be found in the *New Casebook,* edited by David Punter (see **Further reading**).

forgiveness at the religious level; and through selfishness, possessiveness and jealousy at the personal and psychological level.

In Blake, though – and this is what makes some of the *Songs*, as well as most of his other work, so complex – these levels cannot be separated out. We hear in the famous phrase from 'London' of 'mind-forg'd manacles' (line 8); but the brilliance of this phrase lies in its double meaning. On the one hand, we could say that the 'minds' that forge these manacles are the minds of other people; when we observe the inhumanity of urban life we are seeing the imposition of some people's will upon others, or, to put it another way, we are witnessing the suppression of healthy individual life by an ideology comprised of work, power and repression. But it is *at the same time* true that the mind that places these shackles upon us is, in an important sense, our own. Again to use a more modern terminology, we could say that what Blake shows us is not only the forces of violence at work in society and the economy; he also shows us the processes of *internalisation* by means of which we absorb these forces inside ourselves and accept them without question, an acceptance which kills off the all-important development of the imagination inside us.

In some of these respects, it is appropriate to see Blake as a **Romantic** poet. Most of the other major Romantics – Wordsworth, Coleridge, Shelley, Keats – share Blake's distrust of the forces abroad in contemporary society: they too detect an increasing mechanisation in the world around them, and they too recommend a reconsideration of a more 'innocent' state as part of the solution to the problem. Yet in none of these other writers, with the possible exception of Wordsworth, do we find quite the level of *detail* in the description of everyday city life. This is, of course, partly because Blake knew everyday life and its pressures better than they. He came from a lower social class than any of them, and he was under considerably greater pressure to earn his living than any of them. The 'escape to the country' was not for him remotely financially viable. It could also be argued that he was the most politically radical of them, with the possible exception of Shelley. Certainly in comparison with Wordsworth and Coleridge, his two most near contemporaries, he kept his faith more consistently with the revolutionary principle of those early years when all three of them

CONTEXT

For all his life, Blake earned his living as an engraver, but this was a trade that was disappearing as a result of technological developments.

were drastically affected by the extraordinary events of the French Revolution of 1789, even if for various complicated reasons his later poetry became far more obscure than the *Songs*.

TECHNIQUES

It is fair to say that the *Songs* are quite different *poetically* from anything the **Romantics** wrote. It is true that the form of the **ballad** was popular among the Romantics, trying as they were to find a kind of poetry which was freed from the formal constraints of classic eighteenth-century poetry; but nowhere in the balladic poems of the other Romantics do we find quite the terseness of form, the extreme compression of the best of the *Songs*, and nowhere, not even in Wordsworth who shared with Blake an intense respect for childhood and its perceptions, do we find the strange courage that enabled him to write and, in his own peculiar way, publish poems like the simpler of the *Songs of Innocence*. The nearest equivalents to which we can point are the *Lyrical Ballads* (1798) of Wordsworth and Coleridge, and every student of Blake should read them for comparative purposes, but what the reader will find is that though the *Lyrical Ballads* often and very brilliantly represent for us some form of childhood experience, nowhere do they *impersonate* the voice of the child in quite the way Blake manages.

Yet even to use the term 'impersonate' is to do the *Songs of Innocence* a disservice; for it seems clear that Blake was not 'putting on' a voice in these poems; rather he was one of those rare artists who still had inside him the voice of childhood and was able, from time to time, to bring it forth in an unforced fashion, and this is again one of the elements that makes the *Songs*, considering now the two volumes together, so powerful. For the questions we are induced to ask, about man's inhumanity to man, while reading the *Songs of Experience* are rendered vastly more poignant by the way that Blake has uniquely introduced us to the voices of precisely the children who exist as the subjects of, and subject to, a world of suffering; or, to put it another way, the 'experienced' 'Nurses Song' is inseparable from its 'innocent' counterpart, and gathers its force from the pain of the contrast between the two.

CHECK THE NET
You can find plenty of ballads and histories of the ballad on the Net.

QUESTION
In what senses is it helpful to think of Blake as a Romantic poet?

Yet all of this Blake achieves without any obviously striking innovation in poetic terms: rather, his uniqueness consists in the way in which, as we have seen, he brings into the 'official' world of poetry a range of 'unofficial' voices – the ballad, the hymn, the nursery rhyme – and twists them in such a way as to allow them to incorporate new meanings. But within these forms, his mastery is complete: his handling of rhythm and metre, his deployment of rhyme, are all the more remarkable for the simplicity of the language he uses – although there may be a few words in the *Songs* which are not familiar to the contemporary reader, this is only because of the passage of time, and it is safe to say that any of Blake's contemporaries, regardless of their educational and social background, would have immediately understood the words, even if the structure of Blake's thought might have remained elusive.

I say 'would have' because it is, finally, important to remind ourselves of one important fact, which is that, entirely unlike his Romantic contemporaries, all of whom were, after their own fashion, remarkably successful self-publicists, Blake had very little reputation in his own lifetime, and such as he did have was largely based on his apparent eccentricity rather than his art. Was Blake mad? This was a question which absorbed earlier generations of critics, and one which, of course, we are still free to discuss, despite recent critical thinking on the **'death of the author'**; but perhaps the most we can say is this: if Blake was mad, then he was so because of his remarkable clarity of perception, his intransigent insistence on what was wrong with the world as he saw it; and we may be inclined to conclude that the real question is not about Blake's madness but about the madness of the world around him, a world which, of course, was seeing precisely the major economic and social changes which have to a large extent produced the world we live in today.

CONTEXT
The most significant, relevant hymn-writer was Isaac Watts.

 CHECK THE FILM
A film in which Blake plays a large, if mysterious, part is *Dead Man Walking*, directed by Jim Jarmusch, with Johnny Depp.

PART FOUR

CRITICAL HISTORY

HIS FIRST FOLLOWERS

It is hard to consider the critical history of the *Songs* separately from the more general critical history of Blake's works. As I have said above, he was little known in his lifetime. He held one exhibition of his paintings, at his own expense, but it was greeted with incomprehension and bewilderment in most circles. He made copies of some of his illuminated works for his friends, and even sold a few of them, but he was part of no literary scene and had, at least for most of his life, no circle of like-minded friends among whom he could talk about his work.

CHECK THE BOOK

The most recent biography of Blake is Gerald E. Bentley's *The Stranger from Paradise: A Biography of William Blake* (see **Further reading**).

But his fame started to grow shortly before his death, and during the nineteenth century this gradually increased. One crucial moment in this ascent to public view was the 'adoption' of his work by the Rossettis, who tried, with limited success, to see in him a precursor of the Pre-Raphaelite movement. The first substantial critical essay on him was written quite late in the nineteenth century by the poet Swinburne, and it remains an acute and enthusiastic piece of writing.

Later still his work found a great admirer in W.B. Yeats, who, with his colleague E.J. Ellis, published a partial annotated edition. But again, this is a peculiar piece of work: Yeats and Ellis were primarily interested in the tradition of Renaissance magic, and they claimed to have found in Blake a bearer of the magical and Neoplatonic ideas that informed that tradition. Certainly Blake was familiar with some aspects of this tradition, and the much more recent work of Kathleen Raine follows through this familiarity in enormous detail; but at the same time this was a further attempt to force Blake into a straitjacket, and like all such attempts it met with limited success.

NORTHROP FRYE V. DAVID ERDMAN

Through the twentieth century, Blake's fame has consistently risen, to the point where he is now regarded as one of the major poets of the turn of the eighteenth and nineteenth centuries; but it is noteworthy that debates and discussions on the meaning and significance of his poetry continue to the present day. Perhaps a sense of these differences of opinion can best be conveyed by alluding to two of Blake's major twentieth-century critics, Northrop Frye and David Erdman.

Frye's massive and brilliant book on Blake, *Fearful Symmetry* (1947), sets out to show the complexities and symmetries of Blake's mythic system, and in doing so compares it with other mythic systems, classical and Judaeo-Christian. In the course of this book, Frye says many incisive things about Blake, and in particular he sets out the underlying scheme of the Prophetic Books intricately and clearly. If we were to turn, however, from this book to Erdman's *Blake: Prophet against Empire* (1969), it is hard to believe that we are talking about the same writer. Erdman's reading of Blake is entirely as an historical and political commentator: he traces, in the Prophetic Books in particular but also throughout Blake's writing, a vast wealth of historical references – to events during, for example, the American and French Revolutions – and demonstrates for us how remarkably closely in touch Blake kept with the happenings of his times.

OTHER TWENTIETH-CENTURY CRITICISM

Following from these two important works, there have been a wealth of critics and scholars who have looked at Blake from the **mythopoeic** or historical perspective; but there has also been a mass of criticism from other directions and angles, and it will be useful to lay out some of the directions in which Blake criticism has proceeded over recent years.

Accepting that Blake was a political radical, for example, throws up some significant contradictions in his work, and one which is much talked about today is in the field of gender politics. On the one hand, Blake writes a great deal about sexual liberation, by which he means the freedom of individuals, of whatever gender, to pursue their own desires. But, on the other, he also talks a lot about the evil represented by the 'female will', as though this will were

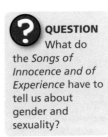

QUESTION
What do the *Songs of Innocence and of Experience* have to tell us about gender and sexuality?

responsible for humanity's downfall. Does he mean by this to indict women, or does he mean to point to a certain restriction of desire which is endemic to the human condition? The question remains open or, perhaps better, hotly contested.

As do many other questions. To take another example, to say that Blake is a radical is obviously in itself an insufficient statement. What were the political limits on that radicalism? How far did he believe it right for the individual to go in the course of resisting pressure from the authorities? We know that Blake, although he observed events around him with a minute eye and was, at least at times, not afraid of saying where his sympathies lay, was nonetheless not a member of any political movement. Was this due to fear, or was it because he saw the role of the poet as working entirely in the field of the imagination rather than engaging in practical activism?

CHECK THE BOOK

The most useful edition of the whole of Blake's poetry is *The Complete Poems*, edited by W.H. Stevenson (see **Further reading**).

To turn in more detail to the *Songs* themselves, here we find a vast range of recent criticism, and again we may identify some specific sources of current critical controversy. We may take as an example the *Songs of Innocence*. In what sense and to what extent are these held together by a common narrative perspective? Many of these *Songs* do appear genuinely innocent, in the sense that we feel that the reader is enjoined to share their celebration of nature and their imaginative delight in human aspiration; but in others, we uneasily sense a certain **irony** creeping in, as though the voice of innocence is itself unstable and always ready to be undercut by a different apprehension of the world.

Or, to take another more specific example, what might we learn by considering the relation between the two 'Nurse's Songs'? Clearly the perspective of the 'experienced' song seems jaundiced when compared with the delight felt by the 'innocent' nurse in her charges' play; but are we then meant to blame the second nurse for this falling away from innocence, or are we meant to see her too as a victim of a wider state of human downfall? We can then broaden this question into one which is relevant to all of us, particularly now, at a time when, for example, the criminal's responsibility for his or her own actions is everywhere a subject of debate: to what extent are individuals responsible for what they do, or are we always at the mercy of larger forces which effectively dictate our lives?

Blake seems to advocate free will, but this view is not wholly borne out by the structure of his longer poems; for if what is really happening in the world is a cosmic battle between forces of good and evil, then how can we as relatively powerless individuals escape being merely pawns in this much larger game? Besides which, what exactly, in Blake, *is* evil? 'Sooner murder an infant in its cradle', he says in one of the most notorious of his Proverbs of Hell, 'than nurse unacted desires'. We may see this as a plea for the liberation of desire; but as with all such pleas, admirable as they may be, we are forced to ask how far such a view can go. Perhaps Blake is here speaking in **metaphor**; indeed, perhaps we rather hope he is; again, perhaps poetry can only speak thus. But even so, we have a right to question how we read the role of liberation in Blake's work.

What, we must also again ask, are innocence and experience? Very occasionally, and not in the *Songs*, Blake invokes a concept of 'organis'd innocence' as the third term to which these two incomplete states point; but what would 'organis'd innocence' be? Is it possible, or even advisable, to retain an 'innocent' perspective in the teeth of life's traumas and troubles? Is there, on the other hand, anything of positive value to be gained from the cynical, world-weary stance which affects some of the 'experienced' poems? Perhaps we have to say at the end of the day that to 'fix' Blake in any one position is a virtually impossible task; but equally, it might be better to say that he presents a continuing challenge to the reader, and this is precisely what makes reading the *Songs*, and Blake's work in general, such a continuingly invigorating experience.

 CHECK THE NET

Try the 'helpfile' at **http://www.newi.ac .uk/rdover/blake** for more information on Blake.

PART FIVE

BACKGROUND

WILLIAM BLAKE'S LIFE

CHECK THE NET

A brief biography can be found at http://www. online-literature. com/blake.

William Blake was born in 1757 in London, where he lived all his life apart from an extended stay in Felpham, near Bognor Regis in Sussex in 1800–3. He died in 1827. He had no formal early education, but studied drawing at a school in the Strand and in the early 1770s became a student, briefly, at the Royal Academy school (where he first met the painter John Flaxman). After this, he was apprenticed to a famous engraver, James Basire. Throughout his life he made his living as an engraver, achieving only modest and intermittent success. He married Catherine Boucher in 1782, but there were no children. About his life we know very little; he kept no diary, and we have very few of his letters. The recent, and excellent, biography by the novelist Peter Ackroyd is by far the best book to flesh out this scanty picture, but much of it is about Blake's times rather than about the poet himself.

We know, from his works, much about his opinions, which were very strongly held. We know, for example, that he was a Christian in the Dissenting tradition which runs back to the seventeenth century; we know that politically he was a radical, sympathetic to the American and French revolutions and to the spirit of freedom wherever he found it. Through most of his life, his paintings and poetry were unknown to most; but in his sixties, he attracted a small circle of younger artists and fellow-visionaries, including Samuel Palmer, John Linnell, John Varley, Edward Calvert and Henry Fuseli, and we may surmise that they at last began to realise the extraordinary genius of his artistic and poetic works.

Today he is known almost as much for his large visionary water-colours illustrating the Book of Job (1820–6), his 102 illustrations of Dante and his colour-printed drawings of biblical subjects, as he is for his poetry.

HIS OTHER LITERARY WORKS

Blake's poetry falls into three main categories. First, there are the lyrics. Of these, the most important are the *Songs of Innocence and of of Experience* themselves, but there are also the earlier poems called *Poetical Sketches* (1769–78), many of which are really experiments in which Blake partly imitates earlier writers (Shakespeare, Thomson and others) as well as a number of other lyrics, some of the most interesting and important of which can be found in what is known as the Pickering Manuscript (*c.*1803). The student of Blake will particularly want to read from this manuscript 'The Mental Traveller' and 'The Crystal Cabinet', which are essential to an understanding of his developing mythology.

This mythology is further elaborated in the second group of poems, which we may refer to as the 'shorter prophecies'. It is important to grasp that when we speak of 'Blake's mythology', as many critics do, we are using a **metaphor**; individuals cannot create mythologies, but Blake's development of a private repertoire of characters and events often has a myth-like ring to it. These shorter prophecies, including *Tiriel* (*c.*1789), *The Book of Thel* (1789), *The Marriage of Heaven and Hell* (*c.*1790–3), *Visions of the Daughters of Albion* (1793), *America* (1793), *Europe* (1794) and the so-called books of the Infernal Bible (*The Book of Urizen* (1794), and *The Song of Los*, *The Book of Ahania* and *The Book of Los* [all 1795]) – all written, as we can see, between 1789 and 1795 – build up this mythology and provide Blake's 'alternative' account of the creation of the world and the nature of God. What they also do is keep in remarkably close touch with the historical events unfolding around him during the closing years of the eighteenth century and the early years of the nineteenth, and they are thus highly complex works which need to be read at mythological, historical and psychological levels.

The third group of poems contains Blake's three long prophecies, *Vala, or, The Four Zoas* (1795–1804), *Milton* (1804–8) and *Jerusalem* (1804–20), the first of which appears never really to have reached final form. These are poems of an **epic** scale, and quite unlike anything to be found elsewhere in British poetry. Between them, they attempt nothing less than a complete account of human history, from its beginnings to the present day; they also represent Blake's attempt to understand contemporary events and incorporate them into his world view, as well as providing us with a psychology which in many ways antedates the work of Freud and other founders of psychoanalysis.

CHECK THE BOOK

The study of Blake's practice as artist and writer has been revolutionised by Joseph Viscomi's *Blake and the Idea of the Book*, 1993 (see **Further reading**).

CHECK THE BOOK

As well as these works, the student may find helpful the short tracts called 'All Religions Are One' and 'There is No Natural Religion' (*c.*1788), which provide useful, if highly complex, accounts of Blake's thinking on such crucial questions as the nature of reason, energy and desire.

Many of the poems are 'illuminated', and ideally they should be read in versions which reproduce the full-colour texts which most properly represent Blake's mixture of poetic and visual creativity; taken together they represent British literature's most determined attempt to create a world system, and although they make for dense reading there are many passages of great beauty to be found among them.

HISTORICAL BACKGROUND

Blake lived through a crucial phase of Western history. Among the major events with which he grapples is the American revolution of 1776, which secured American independence from British rule.

CHECK THE NET

Look up the American and French Revolutions on the Net.

Blake reads this, in *America* and other poems, as a decisive stroke for the freedom and emancipation of the human spirit. The French Revolution, coming thirteen years later, was widely welcomed in the radical artisan circles in which Blake, as a working-class cockney, moved, and Blake welcomed it, beginning what would have been a very large poem, *The French Revolution*, on the subject. Only the first volume of this poem was published, in 1791, and it remains unclear whether Blake desisted from writing it on political grounds or simply because of the pressure of other work.

Blake was politically engaged as few of his contemporary writers were; furthermore, although Wordsworth and Coleridge were both enthusiasts for the European revolutionary spirit when it first appeared, they subsequently retracted their allegiance in a way that Blake never did. He was, we might say, an instinctive radical, with a natural opposition to tyranny wherever he found it and a distrust of authority whether it be represented in kings, priests or even in the very idea of a monolithic deity who rules human affairs. Perhaps the best-known episode of his life was the occasion when he was put on trial for treason, on an apparently trumped-up charge caused by his swearing at a soldier who had strayed into his garden; unimportant as this event may sound (he was not convicted), nevertheless it played a decisive part both in confirming his opposition to the forces of order and also in convincing him that ideas such as his could only in the end be put forth in cryptic, **symbolic** form.

It is also important to bear in mind that the years in which Blake was writing were ones of enormous change in Britain. We speak now of the 'industrial revolution'; while Blake, living in London, did not see a great deal of this at first hand, he was highly and imaginatively aware of how the overall economy of the country was changing and particularly of how social life was becoming increasingly subservient to the demands of wage-labour and the new rules of life enjoined by the factory system.

He saw this, like many other tendencies of his time, as an attempt to restrict human capacity and the freedom of the imagination, and saw his role as contributing to the reinstatement of the imagination as the guiding principle of human affairs. To that extent, certainly, we may see him in terms of the larger movement we refer to as Romanticism; but his class background and his immersion in the London radical tradition set him apart from the other figures in this movement. His political sense was profound; but at the same time he always saw immediate events against a far wider and deeper background, as moments in the general evolution and development of humanity, and thus his poetry attains a cosmic dimension in which individual human battles are always seen as *examples* of a wider perennial battle between the expanding force of energy and the restrictive, numbing, death-dealing force of reason.

CHECK THE BOOK

For further detail, try Nicholas M. Williams' *Ideology and Utopia in the Poetry of William Blake*, 1998 (see **Further reading**).

LITERARY BACKGROUND

The most important thing to grasp about Blake's literary background is that he was self-taught, an autodidact, and as such relied very heavily in literary terms on those texts most available to him. First and foremost among these was the Bible, and it is fair to say that a detailed knowledge of the Bible illuminates the Prophetic Books at every point. Even more particularly, we find images from the Book of Revelation recurring constantly, perhaps especially in *Jerusalem*, and the earlier books of the Infernal Bible were in part Blake's attempt to rewrite the first books of the Old Testament according to his religious beliefs.

Second in importance for the study of Blake is Milton, whom Blake regarded as his predecessor. One of the best known of Blake's statements concerns Milton's *Paradise Lost*, in connection with which he says that Milton was 'of the devil's party without knowing it'; in other words, Milton, who was himself politically a revolutionary, committed a grand but ultimately supremely valuable failure in *Paradise Lost* in that, while claiming to 'justify the ways of God to man', he in fact justified Satan's rebellion against divine tyranny. This kind of rebellion, Blake thought, was always justified; repression, whether it be divine or human, will always breed revolution – as Freud was to say a century later.

CHECK THE NET

One writer whom Blake did read was the Swedish mystic, Emmanuel Swedenborg. Look him up on the Net.

Apart from these great sources, we know little of Blake's reading. We do know that he read various theological works, because we have his annotations to them; we know that he read some Wordsworth, and did not like it very much. We know that he had a pronounced antipathy towards the 'classical', and we may surmise that he would have found the neatness and order of **Augustan** poetry entirely beneath his notice.

In the particular case of Blake, it is at least as important to consider also his antecedents in the visual arts. He saw himself as a follower of Michelangelo, and there is a certain massive, heroic quality to much of his art which attests to this belief; we know too that he thoroughly despised most of his contemporary artists, being especially vituperative about Sir Joshua Reynolds, although this is at least in part a side-effect of his general distaste for 'official art' and the institutions, such as the Royal Academy, which control it.

But his more visionary paintings and drawings have in fact very few antecedents; in quite what sense Blake actually saw visions remains, and probably will always remain, unclear, but certainly pictures like, for example, the celebrated 'Ghost of a Flea' have evidently been done from the inner eye rather than from any particular convictions about what painting ought to be. In both literary and visual terms, Blake remains very much his own man: anti-classical, anti-official, certainly, but at the same time too deeply rooted both, paradoxically, in his own imagination *and* in his everyday environment to warrant any easy assimilation into the category of the **Romantic**.

Perhaps one of the most typical assessments of Blake's relations to his literary and painterly antecedents remains that version which is accurately summarised by Northrop Frye:

> Many students of literature or painting must have felt that Blake's relation to those arts is a somewhat quizzical one. Critics in both fields insist almost exclusively upon the angularity of his genius. Blake, they tell us, is a mystic enraptured with incommunicable visions, standing apart, a lonely and isolated figure, out of touch with his own age and without influence on the following one. He is an interruption in cultural history, a separable phenomenon.

And yet if that is the case, we have still to ask – as Frye also does – how it can be that this 'isolated' figure can also be seen in a quite different light: as a writer and artist who has, despite all the difficulties, moved to the centre of the stage of British cultural history, and can now be seen as having taken into himself many of the major literary, cultural and theological influences of previous ages, given them an entirely individual twist, and emerged as a thoroughly respected and occasionally virtually sanctified icon of a certain version of 'Britishness' typified by individualism, resistance to authority and stubborn commonsense.

 CHECK THE NET
The largest ever exhibition of Blake's art was mounted at the Tate in 2001. You can still see it at **http://www.tate. org.uk/britain/ exhibitions/blake interactive**.

World events	Blake's life	Literary events
	1757 Birth of Blake in London	
1760 Accession of George III	1767 At drawing school in The Strand	
1764 Invention of Spinning Jenny	1769-78 *Poetical Sketches*	
1768 Royal Academy founded: first president Joshua Reynolds	1770s (early) Becomes student at Royal Academy school	
1770 Cook discovers Australia		
1775 Outbreak of War of American Independence	1774 (c.) Apprenticed to engraver James Basire	1774 Goethe, *The Sorrows of Young Werther*
1778 France allies with American colonies		
1780 The Gordon Riots, London: 'No Popery'		1779 William Cowper and John Newton, *The Olney Hymns*
1783 American Independence is recognised	1782 Marries Catherine Boucher	
1788 George III's first attack of madness	1788 (c.) 'All Religions Are One' and 'There Is No Natural Religion'	1788 Wesley brothers, *A Collection of Hymns and Psalms for the Lord's Day*
1789 Outbreak of French Revolution	1789 *Songs of Innocence*; *The Book of Thel*	1789 Gilbert White, *The Natural History of Selbourne*
	1789 (c.) *Tiriel*	
	1790-3 (c.) *The Marriage of Heaven and Hell*	
	1791 *The French Revolution (vol. 1)*	1791 Thomas Paine, *The Rights of Man*
1792 France is declared a republic	1792 *Song of Liberty*	
1793 Reign of Terror in France	1793 *Visions of the Daughters of Albion; America*	
	1794 *Songs of Experience*; *Europe; The Book of Urizen*	

World events	Blake's life	Literary events
	1795 *The Song of Los; The Book of Ahania; The Book of Los*	
	1795-1804 *Vala, or, The Four Zoas*	1796 Coleridge edits *The Watchman*
1798 Invention of lithography		1798 Wordsworth and Coleridge, *Lyrical Ballads*
	1800 Moves to Felpham and lives under patronage of poet William Hayley	
1803 First railway steam engine	1803 Returns to London	
1804 Napoleon crowned emperor	1804-8 *Milton*	
1805 Battle of Trafalgar	1804-20 *Jerusalem*, including 100 engravings	1811 Jane Austen, *Sense and Sensibility*
1812 Luddite riots	1809 *Descriptive Catalogue of Pictures, Poetical and Historical Inventions*	1812 Lord Byron, *Childe Harold*
	1810 *The Canterbury Pilgrims* (engravings)	1813 Jane Austen, *Pride and Prejudice*
1814 Napoleon abdicates		1814 Shelley, *The Refutation of Deism*
1816 Riots in Britain		1816 Coleridge, *Christabel*
1819 Peterloo massacre. Children under 9 forbidden to work in cotton mills		1817 Keats, *Poems*
		1818 Mary Shelley, *Frankenstein*
1820 George III dies	1820-21 Large watercolours for *Book of Job*	1820 Clare, *Poems*; Shelley, *Prometheus Unbound*
1824 Workers allowed to form unions. Foundation of RSPCA	1824 First meets young visionary painter, Samuel Palmer	
	1826 *Book of Job* engravings	
	1827 Publishes 102 engravings to Dante. Dies	

FURTHER READING

Peter Ackroyd, *Blake*, Sinclair-Stevenson, 1995
  Much the best biography of Blake

Gerald E. Bentley, Jr, ed., *William Blake: The Critical Heritage*, Routledge and Kegan Paul, 1975
  A collection of short criticism on Blake, from his times to our own

Gerald E. Bentley, *The Stranger from Paradise: A Biography of William Blake*, Yale University Press, 2001

Jacob Bronowski, *William Blake and the Age of Revolution*, Routledge and Kegan Paul, 1972
  A revised version of Bronowski's earlier *William Blake 1757–1827: A Man without a Mask*, this book is a simple but trenchant account of Blake's politics

S. Foster Damon, *A Blake Dictionary: The Ideas and Symbols of William Blake*, Brown University Press, 1965
  A rather old but useful reference text

Maurice Eaves, editor, *The Cambridge Companion to William Blake,* Cambridge University Press, 2003

David V. Erdman, *Blake: Prophet against Empire*, rev. edn, Princeton University Press, 1969
  The most wide-ranging account of Blake's historical context and political references

Michael Ferber, *The Social Vision of William Blake*, Princeton University Press, 1985
  A highly readable synthesis of Blake as London craftsman, religious Dissenter and political thinker

Northrop Frye, *Fearful Symmetry: A Study of William Blake*, Princeton University Press, 1947
  A magnificent reading of Blake from a largely mythic perspective

Heather Glen, *Vision and Disenchantment: Blake's* Songs *and Wordsworth's* Lyrical Ballads, Cambridge University Press, 1983
  A highly detailed textual reading which places Blake firmly within a complex cultural history

Nelson Hilton, editor, *Essential Articles for the Study of William Blake, 1970-84*, Archon, 1986

John Holloway, *Blake: the Lyric Poetry,* Edwin Anold, 1990

Geoffrey Keane, editor, *Blake: Complete Writings*, Oxford University Press, 1966

Zachary Leader, *Reading Blake's* Songs, Routledge and Kegan Paul, 1981
An excellent commentary on the *Songs of Innocence and of Experience*

Jon Mee, *Dangerous Enthusiasm: William Blake and the Culture of Radicalism in the 1790s*, Clarendon Press, 1992

W. J. T. Mitchell, *Blake's Composite Art: A Study of the Illuminated Poetry*, Princeton University Press, 1978
Perhaps the most impressive contemporary approach to the complex interweavings of the various art-forms in Blake

Morton D. Paley, *Energy and the Imagination: A Study of the Development of Blake's Thought*, Clarendon Press, 1970
A watershed book which can be seen as inaugurating modern Blake criticism

David Punter, ed., *Blake: The New Casebook*, Macmillan, 1996
Brings together much of the most important recent work on Blake

David Punter, ed., *William Blake: Selected Poetry and Prose*, Routledge, 1988
The edition used in these Notes for all Blake references except the *Songs*

W.H. Stevenson, editor, *Blake: The Complete Poems*, Longman, 1989

E.P. Thompson, *Witness against the Beast: William Blake and the Moral Law*, Cambridge University Press, 1993

Joseph Viscomi, *Blake and the Idea of the Book*, Princeton University Press, 1993

Brenda S. Webster, *Blake's Prophetic Psychology*, Macmillan, 1983
Challenging and thought-provoking

Nicholas M. Williams, *Ideology and Utopia in the Poetry of William Blake*, Cambridge University Press, 1998

alienation the sense of being separated from, or adrift within, one's environment or social context

allegory a narrative written in such a way as to permit two different coherent readings, often marked by simple one-to-one correlation between events and characters

alliteration a sequence of repeated consonantal sounds in a stretch of language

anthropomorphism the attribution of human characteristics to the non-human world, often to animals and other creatures

assonance the correspondence in two words of the stressed vowel and sometimes those which follow

Augustan a term used to refer to the literature of the earlier eighteenth century, which was often seen during the Romantic period as being characterised by a high level of artificiality

ballad a traditional poem or song which tells a story in simple, colloquial language

'death of the author' a body of literary theory, particularly associated with the French critic Roland Barthes, based on the actual absence of the author and his/her intentions from the text

dimeter a line consisting of two metrical feet; rarely used except in conjunction with other line-lengths e.g.,

> Shall shi\ne like the go\ld,
> As I gua\rd o'er the fo\ld

enjambement term which is used to describe a line of poetry which is not end-stopped, and the sentence continues into the next line without punctuation

epic a long narrative poem in elevated style, usually on mythological or heroic themes

interpellation a term, used particularly by the French political thinker Louis Althusser, to describe the way in which we as individuals are 'hailed' or addressed by discourse

interpretation the act of explaining the meaning and effects of a text

irony a very general term descriptive of any piece of speech and writing in which we assume a difference between what is said and what is meant

metaphor probably a condition of all language, metaphor describes the process whereby one thing is described in terms of another

mythopoeia the invention of myth-like systems, usually by poets but sometimes in other forms of writing

Neoclassical term usually used to describe those forms of eighteenth-century writing that modelled themselves on classical, and especially Latin, forms and conventions. The poets Alexander Pope, John Dryden and Oliver Goldsmith are generally included in this category, as are prose writers such as Jonathan Swift and Joseph Addison

pastoral a kind of writing which idealises rural life and implicitly condemns modernity and change

pentameter a line consisting of five metrical feet; when these feet are basically iambic in form, the most common line-form in British poetry e.g.,

I kno\w a ba\nk whereo\n the wi\ld thyme gro\ws

persona when the author uses a point of view which is clearly not his or hers for the purpose of narration

quatrain a stanza consisting of four lines e.g.,

Tyger, Tyger, burning bright,
In the forests of the night;
What immortal hand or eye,
Could frame thy fearful symmetry?

rhapsody the outpouring of emotion, sometimes without much regard for formal constraints

rhetoric originally the art of persuading an audience, the term is now often used to cover the whole range of literary and linguistic devices

Romantic term used to refer to the main literary movement of the period roughly from 1789 to 1830, among whose principal English writers were Wordsworth, Coleridge, Byron, Keats and Shelley

satire literature that explores vice or folly and makes them appear ridiculous; usually morally censorious

LITERARY TERMS

symbol in a symbol different things are joined into one; some symbols may be invented by authors, others may have general cultural or mythic valency e.g.,

> the lamb symbolises innocence; in Church symbolism it also symbolises God in human form, and sacrifice

tetrameter a line consisting of four metrical feet, e.g.,

> Love se\eketh no\t Itse\lf to ple\ase

transferred epithet an adjective or description transferred meaningfully from one noun to another in a particular phrase, line or sentence e.g.,

> Little Lamb
> Here I am,
> Come and lick
> My white neck.

trimeter a line consisting of three metrical feet e.g.,

> Lo\st in des\art wi\ld
> Is\ your li\ttle chi\ld

David Punter is Professor of English Studies at the University of Bristol. Among his many books are *The Romantic Unconscious* (1989) and *The Literature of Terror* (2 vols, 1996). He has also edited *William Blake: Selected Poetry and Prose* (Routledge, 1988) and *Blake: The New Casebook* (Macmillan, 1996).

General editors

Martin Gray, former Head of the Department of English Studies at the University of Stirling, and of Literary Studies at the University of Luton

Professor A. N. Jeffares, Emeritus Professor of English, University of Stirling

NOTES

NOTES

NOTES

Maya Angelou
I Know Why the Caged Bird Sings

Jane Austen
Pride and Prejudice

Alan Ayckbourn
Absent Friends

Elizabeth Barrett Browning
Selected Poems

Robert Bolt
A Man for All Seasons

Harold Brighouse
Hobson's Choice

Charlotte Brontë
Jane Eyre

Emily Brontë
Wuthering Heights

Shelagh Delaney
A Taste of Honey

Charles Dickens
David Copperfield
Great Expectations
Hard Times
Oliver Twist

Roddy Doyle
Paddy Clarke Ha Ha Ha

George Eliot
Silas Marner
The Mill on the Floss

Anne Frank
The Diary of a Young Girl

William Golding
Lord of the Flies

Oliver Goldsmith
She Stoops to Conquer

Willis Hall
The Long and the Short and the Tall

Thomas Hardy
Far from the Madding Crowd
The Mayor of Casterbridge
Tess of the d'Urbervilles
The Withered Arm and other Wessex Tales

L.P. Hartley
The Go-Between

Seamus Heaney
Selected Poems

Susan Hill
I'm the King of the Castle

Barry Hines
A Kestrel for a Knave

Louise Lawrence
Children of the Dust

Harper Lee
To Kill a Mockingbird

Laurie Lee
Cider with Rosie

Arthur Miller
The Crucible
A View from the Bridge

Robert O'Brien
Z for Zachariah

Frank O'Connor
My Oedipus Complex and Other Stories

George Orwell
Animal Farm

J.B. Priestley
An Inspector Calls
When We Are Married

Willy Russell
Educating Rita
Our Day Out

J.D. Salinger
The Catcher in the Rye

William Shakespeare
Henry IV Part I
Henry V
Julius Caesar
Macbeth
The Merchant of Venice
A Midsummer Night's Dream
Much Ado About Nothing
Romeo and Juliet
The Tempest
Twelfth Night

George Bernard Shaw
Pygmalion

Mary Shelley
Frankenstein

R.C. Sherriff
Journey's End

Rukshana Smith
Salt on the snow

John Steinbeck
Of Mice and Men

Robert Louis Stevenson
Dr Jekyll and Mr Hyde

Jonathan Swift
Gulliver's Travels

Robert Swindells
Daz 4 Zoe

Mildred D. Taylor
Roll of Thunder, Hear My Cry

Mark Twain
Huckleberry Finn

James Watson
Talking in Whispers

Edith Wharton
Ethan Frome

William Wordsworth
Selected Poems

A Choice of Poets

Mystery Stories of the Nineteenth Century including The Signalman

Nineteenth Century Short Stories

Poetry of the First World War

Six Women Poets

For the AQA Anthology:

Duffy and Armitage & Pre-1914 Poetry

Heaney and Clarke & Pre-1914 Poetry

Poems from Different Cultures

Margaret Atwood
Cat's Eye
The Handmaid's Tale

Jane Austen
Emma
Mansfield Park
Persuasion
Pride and Prejudice
Sense and Sensibility

Alan Bennett
Talking Heads

William Blake
Songs of Innocence and of Experience

Charlotte Brontë
Jane Eyre
Villette

Emily Brontë
Wuthering Heights

Angela Carter
Nights at the Circus

Geoffrey Chaucer
The Franklin's Prologue and Tale
The Merchant's Prologue and Tale
The Miller's Prologue and Tale
The Prologue to the Canterbury Tales
The Wife of Bath's Prologue and Tale

Samuel Coleridge
Selected Poems

Joseph Conrad
Heart of Darkness

Daniel Defoe
Moll Flanders

Charles Dickens
Bleak House
Great Expectations
Hard Times

Emily Dickinson
Selected Poems

John Donne
Selected Poems

Carol Ann Duffy
Selected Poems

George Eliot
Middlemarch
The Mill on the Floss

T.S. Eliot
Selected Poems
The Waste Land

F. Scott Fitzgerald
The Great Gatsby

E.M. Forster
A Passage to India

Brian Friel
Translations

Thomas Hardy
Jude the Obscure
The Mayor of Casterbridge
The Return of the Native
Selected Poems
Tess of the d'Urbervilles

Seamus Heaney
Selected Poems from 'Opened Ground'

Nathaniel Hawthorne
The Scarlet Letter

Homer
The Iliad
The Odyssey

Aldous Huxley
Brave New World

Kazuo Ishiguro
The Remains of the Day

Ben Jonson
The Alchemist

James Joyce
Dubliners

John Keats
Selected Poems

Philip Larkin
The Whitsun Weddings and Selected Poems

Christopher Marlowe
Doctor Faustus
Edward II

Arthur Miller
Death of a Salesman

John Milton
Paradise Lost Books I & II

Toni Morrison
Beloved

George Orwell
Nineteen Eighty-Four

Sylvia Plath
Selected Poems

Alexander Pope
Rape of the Lock & Selected Poems

William Shakespeare
Antony and Cleopatra
As You Like It
Hamlet
Henry IV Part I
King Lear
Macbeth
Measure for Measure
The Merchant of Venice
A Midsummer Night's Dream
Much Ado About Nothing
Othello
Richard II
Richard III
Romeo and Juliet
The Taming of the Shrew
The Tempest
Twelfth Night
The Winter's Tale

George Bernard Shaw
Saint Joan

Mary Shelley
Frankenstein

Jonathan Swift
Gulliver's Travels and A Modest Proposal

Alfred Tennyson
Selected Poems

Virgil
The Aeneid

Alice Walker
The Color Purple

Oscar Wilde
The Importance of Being Earnest

Tennessee Williams
A Streetcar Named Desire
The Glass Menagerie

Jeanette Winterson
Oranges Are Not the Only Fruit

John Webster
The Duchess of Malfi

Virginia Woolf
To the Lighthouse

William Wordsworth
The Prelude and Selected Poems

W.B. Yeats
Selected Poems

Metaphysical Poets

THE ULTIMATE WEB SITE FOR THE ULTIMATE LITERATURE GUIDES

At York Notes we believe in helping you achieve exam success. Log on to **www.yorknotes.com** and see how we have made revision even easier, with over 300 titles available to download twenty-four hours a day. The downloads have lots of additional features such as pop-up boxes providing instant glossary definitions, user-friendly links to every part of the guide, and scanned illustrations offering visual appeal. All you need to do is log on to **www.yorknotes.com** and download the books you need to help you achieve exam success.

KEY FEATURES:

Details on how York Notes can help you

Menu Bar to help you find your way around the site

Details on how to download York Notes

Quick Search facility to help you find the titles you need

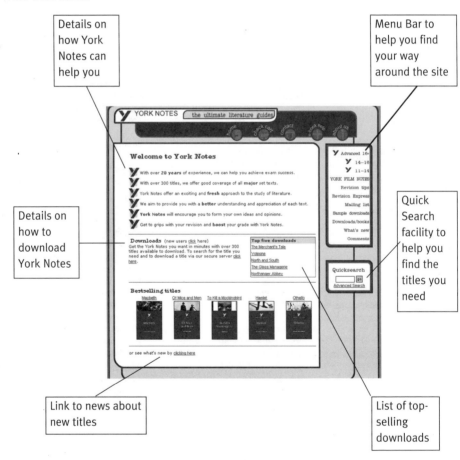

Link to news about new titles

List of top-selling downloads